O Timothy!

Guard the Deposit of Faith

—〰—

By Michael P. McKeating

Nihil Obstat:
Rev. Peter Drilling, Th.D.
Censor Liborum

Imprimatur:
Most. Rev. Edward U. Kmiec, D.D.
Bishop of Buffalo
March 7, 2007

The "nihil obstat" and "imprimatur" are official declarations that the book or pamphlet are free of doctrinal or moral error. No implication is contained therein that those who have granted the "nihil obstat" and "imprimatur" agree with the content, opinions or statements expressed.

O Timothy! Guard the Deposit of Faith
By Michael P. McKeating

Printed in the United States of America

ISBN 978-1-60266-426-5

Unless otherwise indicated, Bible quotations are taken from the *Revised Standard Version,* Catholic Edition, Copyright © 1946, 1952, 1971 by the Division of Christian Education of the National Council of Churches of Christ in the USA. Used by permission. All rights reserved.

Excerpts from the English translation of the Catechism of the catholic church for the United States of America copyright © 1994, United States catholic Conference, Inc.—Libreria Editrice Vaticana. English translation of the Catechism of the catholic church Modifications from the Editio Typica copyright ©1997, United States catholic conference, Inc. Libreria Editrice Vaticana. Used with permission.

Library of Congress Cataloging-in-Publication Data

McKeating, Michael P. 1944

www.xulonpress.com

ACKNOWLEDGMENTS

—∿∿—

This book is dedicated to my professors in the Graduate Theology Department at Franciscan University of Steubenville, particularly Professors Scott Hahn, Regis Martin, Andrew Minto, Mark Miravale, Barbara Morgan, Bob Rice, Alan Schreck, Scott Sollom, Fr. Dan Pattee, T.O.R., and in a very special way, Fr. Michael Scanlan, TO.R., Chancellor and President Emeritus of Franciscan University, whose foresight, wisdom and docility to the Holy Spirit has molded Franciscan University into the beacon of dynamic orthodoxy that it is for the Catholic Church today.

TABLE OF CONTENTS

INTRODUCTION

—𝔪—

This book is addressed to catechists—but catechists in the broadest sense of the word. The word "catechesis" comes from two Greek words which mean "to echo down." The job of catechists is to "echo down" the Deposit of Faith which was handed down from Jesus to the apostles, and from the apostles to their successors—the bishops down through the ages. So in this sense, all priests, deacons, paid and volunteer religion teachers, parents and godparents, even grandparents and siblings, are catechists; and in this sense they are the target audience of this book.

This book is not intended as a catechetical manual, nor as a curriculum, nor as a syllabus. The purpose is much more modest, but nonetheless important. It is to convey to the reader certain things which a catechist needs to know in order to do his or her job properly, but which are seldom taught in religious studies programs, or even in seminaries.

In many universities and seminaries and ministry formation programs today, students are taught the theories of theologians, or theories concerning educational techniques or methods. They are taught to ask their students opinions about God, to facilitate the students' looking within themselves to find who God is for them. But too often they are not taught to hand on the doctrine of the faith in a systematic, coherent, integral way; the way Jesus taught the Apostles, and the way the Apostles taught the Fathers.

Many catechists today do not know what the Deposit of Faith is, what the Rule of Faith is, what the Standard of Faith is, what the Deposit of Grace is. They do not know what Jesus was doing during the Forty Days, or even what Forty Days we're talking about, or why they are important at all. They do not know how to tell The Story, or even the importance of telling The Story. And they do not know or clearly understand the three ways in which the Church can exercise the charism of infallibility through the Magisterium.

If I had a dollar for every time I have heard it said, even by those who should know better, that the Pope only speaks infallibly when he speaks *ex cathedra*, I would be very rich indeed. And yet, such a statement is manifestly false, and it is causing grave scandal by misleading the faithful. Those of us who have the responsibility for handing on the faith have an awesome responsibility to hand it on correctly. I hope that this book will help us to do that.

CHAPTER ONE

THE DEPOSIT OF FAITH

—ᵡᵡᵡ—

O Timothy, guard what has been entrusted to you.

Avoid the godless chatter and

contradictions of what

Is falsely called knowledge,

for by professing it some

Have missed the mark as regards the faith.

1 Timothy 6:20.

The "Deposit of Faith" is the name given to the body of doctrine which is the subject of all catechesis. It is that which is taught. The Deposit of Faith is the great storehouse of what we need to know for our salvation, and that we would not know if God had not revealed it to us.

The Deposit of Faith is that which must be believed by every Catholic. The source of the Deposit of Faith is Jesus, the Divine Teacher. He taught it to the Apostles through his words and deeds during his public ministry. But he particularly brought it together, summarized it and hammered it home during that gigantic review course which comprised the Forty Days between his Resurrection and Ascension.

The Deposit of Faith is fixed. It is firm. It is sure. It is the bedrock of what we believe, what we do, what we live as Catholics. It does not change. Our understanding of it can develop, but it does not change. There has never been a doctrine which was part of the Deposit of Faith in one time, and not in another; and there never will be.

Nor is it ever added to. There is no new doctrine, because the source of doctrine is Jesus Christ himself, his words and deeds. Although some theologians speak of the "development of doctrine," this never means that there are new doctrines. The term "development of doctrine" refers to a deeper, richer or fuller understanding of truths which have already been revealed by Jesus Christ through his words and deeds having an inner unity. The Church teaches infallibly that public revelation was closed with the death of the last Apostle, and that there will be no new revelation before the Second Coming of Christ.[1]

It is called the "Deposit" of Faith because the word used in the New Testament to convey this concept was παραθέκέ (paratheke), which meant "deposit." The New Testament Lexicon defines *paratheke* as:

1. a deposit, a trust or thing consigned to one's faithful keeping.

    a) used of the correct knowledge and pure doctrine of the gospel, to be held firmly and faithfully, and to be conscientiously delivered to others.

Unfortunately, some modern translations of the bible translate *paratheke* in ways that are less mean-

---

[1] *Dei Verbum, #4.*

ingful or precise. Some translate it with the English word *treasure.* Although it is a treasure, that word does not convey all the nuances of the word *deposit,* particularly the important idea that it is something to be held in trust. The NAB translates it in that key passage, 1 Timothy 6:20, which sets forth the mission of all clerics and catechists, thus:

O Timothy, hold fast to *that which has been entrusted to you.*

Although *that which has been entrusted to you* does convey the meaning of *paratheke,* it is using seven words to translate one. Throughout this work we shall use the word *deposit*, which is familiar to many because it has been used down through the centuries in Magisterial documents to refer to that body of teaching which was received from Jesus, through the Apostles, and is to be guarded and handed on by all those entrusted with the teaching office.

For example, when Pope John XXIII called the Second Vatican Council, he said the principal task entrusted to the Council would be "to guard and present better the precious *deposit* of Christian doctrine in order to make it more accessible to the Christian faithful and to all people of good will."[2]

Then again, thirty years later in the Papal Bull issued on October 11, 1992, promulgating the new Catechism of the Catholic Church (*CCC*), a Bull which he entitled *The Deposit of Faith* (*Fidei Depositum*), Pope John Paul II said:

Guarding the Deposit of the Faith is the mission which the Lord entrusted to his Church, and which she fulfills in every age.[3]

St. Irenaeus of Lyons, that great Doctor of the Church who in many ways is the father of catechetics, said:

---

[2] Pope John XXIII, Discourse at the opening of the Second Vatican Ecumenical Council, October 11, 1962: AAS 54 (1962) pp. 788-91.

[3] *Catechism of the Catholic Church,* p. 1.

We guard with care the faith that we have received from the Church, for without ceasing, under the action of God's Spirit, this deposit of great price, as if in an excellent vessel, is constantly being renewed and causes the very vessel that contains it to be renewed.[4]

The Catechism, in Article 2, which deals with Transmission of Divine Revelation, teaches:

The apostles entrusted the "Sacred deposit" of the faith (the *depositum fidei)*, contained in Sacred Scripture and Tradition, to the whole of the Church. "By adhering to [this heritage] the entire holy people, united to its pastors, remains always faithful to the teaching of the apostles, to the brotherhood, to the breaking of the bread and the prayers. So, in maintaining, practicing and professing the faith that has been handed on, there should be a

---

[4] St. Irenaeus, Adv. Haeres, 3,24.

remarkable harmony between the bishops and the faithful.[5]

So what is the Deposit of Faith? Of what does it consist? New catechists sometimes ask that question as if they expect to find a pamphlet listing the Deposit of Faith in numbered paragraphs. In a sense there is. It is called the *Catechism.* A good working definition of the Deposit of Faith is that it is:

Sacred Scripture + Sacred Tradition +
The Magisterium

The Magisterium is the teaching office of the Church. The Second Vatican Council's *Dogmatic Constitution on Divine Revelation (Dei Verbum)* teaches:

Sacred tradition and Sacred Scripture form one sacred deposit of the word of God,

---

[5] *CCC, #84.*

committed to the Church. Holding fast to this deposit the entire holy people united with their shepherds remain always steadfast in the teaching of the Apostles, in the common life, in the breaking of the bread and in prayers (see Acts 2:42, Greek text), so that holding to, practicing and professing the heritage of the faith, it becomes on the part of the bishops and faithful a single common effort.

But the task of authentically interpreting the word of God, whether written or handed on, has been entrusted exclusively to the living teaching office of the Church, whose authority is exercised in the name of Jesus Christ. This teaching office is not above the word of God, but serves it, teaching only what has been handed on, listening to it devoutly, guarding it scrupulously and explaining it faithfully in accord with a divine commission and with the help of the Holy Spirit, it draws from this one deposit of faith everything which it presents for belief as divinely revealed.

It is clear, therefore, that Sacred Tradition, Sacred Scripture and the teaching authority of the Church, in accord with God's most wise design, are so linked and joined together that one cannot stand without the others, and that all together and each in its own way under the action of the one Holy Spirit contribute effectively to the salvation of souls.[6]

It would not be correct to hold, as do fundamentalists, that the Deposit of Faith is Sacred Scripture alone, for there are revealed truths, necessary for salvation, which are not explicitly contained in scripture. Nor would it be correct to say that Sacred Scripture and Sacred Tradition, without the Magisterium, comprise the Deposit of Faith, for without the Magisterium we would have no sure and reliable conduit of Sacred

---

[6] *Dei Verbum, #10.*

Tradition, no yardstick for determining what it contained.

For example, the great Christological debate, which occupied the entire Fourth and much of the Fifth Centuries, centering on the person and nature of Jesus, could not have been resolved without a firm and decisive exercise of the Magisterium. It could not be resolved based on Scripture alone, because Scripture does not explicitly address it. It could not be resolved based on Tradition alone, because Tradition was still developing. It required an exercise of a Council of the Church, the Council of Nicea in 325 A.D., to develop the concept of ***homoousios,*** the idea that although Jesus has two natures, one human and the other divine, he is one person, and that person is *homo* (one) *ousios* (essence, substance, being) with the Father. Through the exercise of the Magisterium by the Council of Nicea, the doctrine of *homoousios* became part of the Deposit of Faith, although it required several more Councils to resolve further nuances in the great Christological debate.

Today this resolution, which is contained in the Creed of Nicea-Constantinople which is recited at the Mass, is accepted by virtually all who call themselves Christian.

The content of the Deposit of Faith is that body of doctrine which Jesus handed on to the Apostles, and commanded them to hand on to us, for the sake of our salvation. Much of it is contained in Sacred Scripture, but not all. Some doctrines are alluded to or contained in seminal form in Scripture, but not explicitly developed. At the end of St. John's Gospel he says:

Now Jesus did many other signs in the presence of his disciples, which are not written in this book; but these are written that you may believe that Jesus is the Christ, the Son of God, and that believing you may have life in his name.[7]

---

[7] John 20:20.

So if the entirety of the Deposit of Faith is not contained in Sacred Scripture, how did we get the rest of it? Through the oral teaching of the Apostles, which has been handed down through their successor bishops, and their assistants, the priests, deacons and catechists, to the present day. Jesus had a plan for our salvation. The plan was that he would hand on the Deposit of Faith to the Apostles, and they would hand it on to us, until the end of time. This was "Plan A." There was no "Plan B." The salvation of the world depends on the bishops, priests, deacons and catechists faithfully handing on the Deposit of Faith which they received from Jesus through the Apostles. The Catechism says this about the "handing on" of the Deposit:

> The apostles entrusted the "sacred deposit" of the faith (the *depositum fidei*), contained in Sacred Scripture and Tradition, to the whole of the Church. "By adhering to [this heritage] the entire holy people united to its pastors,

remains always faithful to the teaching of the apostles, to the brotherhood, to the breaking of the bread and the prayers. So in maintaining, practicing and professing the faith that has been handed on, there should always be a remarkable harmony between the bishops and the faithful."[8]

In the *Compendium to the Catechism of the Catholic Church,* published by Pope Benedict XVI on June 28, 2005, summarizing the *Catechism* itself as well as the universal tradition of the Church, the issue of who has the authority to interpret the *Deposit of Faith* is specifically addressed. The *Compendium* teaches:

The task of giving an authentic interpretation of the deposit of faith has been entrusted to the living teaching office of the Church alone, that is, to the successor of Peter, the Bishop

---

[8] *CCC, #84.*

of Rome, and to the bishops in communion with him. To this Magisterium, which in the service of the Word of God enjoys a certain charism of truth, belongs also the task of defining dogmas which are formulations of truth contained in divine revelation. This authority of the Magisterium also extends to those truths necessarily connected with Revelation.[9]

It is important here to pay particular attention to the verb which is nearly always used in Scripture, Tradition and Magisterial statements when speaking about the transmission of the Deposit of Faith. The word used in Scripture, in the original Greek, is παραδωσισ (paradosis). It is translated into English as "to hand on." It does not mean to paraphrase, or modify, or summarize; it means to hand on intact, without addition, subtraction, or change. A few examples from Sacred Scripture will suffice to illustrate:

---

[9] *Compendium to the Catechism of the Catholic Church, #16.*

For I received from the Lord what I also handed on to you, that the Lord Jesus, on the night he was handed over, took bread...
— *1 Corinthians 11:23.*

For I handed on to you as of first importance what I also received...
1 Corinthians 15:34

Since many have undertaken to compile a narrative of the events which have been fulfilled among us, just as those who were eyewitnesses from the beginning and ministers of the word have handed them down to us.
— *Luke 1:1-2.*

So then, brethren, stand firm and hold to the traditions which you were taught by us, either by word of mouth or by letter.
2 Thessalonians 2:15.

St. Irenaeus of Lyons, the great Father of the Church who lived in the Second Century, is often regarded as the Father of Catechetics, which is the art of handing on the faith through oral teaching. He was but one generation removed from the apostles. He was a disciple of St. Polycarp of Smyrna, who himself studied at the feet of St. John the Evangelist, the beloved disciple to whom Jesus entrusted the care of his Blessed Mother. He was born in Smyrna, in what is now Turkey in about 130 A.D., and after being ordained by St. Polycarp, he was sent to Gaul, eventually becoming bishop of Lyons. He was tireless and single-minded in his defense of the Deposit of Faith. His most famous written work, *Against Heresies,* teaches us much of what we know about catechetical content and method in apostolic and patristic times. St. Irenaeus said:

We guard with great care the faith that we have received from the church, for without ceasing, under the action of God's Spirit, this deposit of great price, as if in an excellent vessel, is constantly being renewed and causes the very vessel that contains it to be renewed.[10]

Jesus never wrote a book, and the apostles had little if any access to books. The Deposit of Faith is the Word of God, much of which was scattered throughout the Jewish Scriptures, but which Jesus himself gathered together in a brief, teachable summary and handed on orally to his apostles. Jesus indicated that it was in the nature of a deposit, a trust, when he said:

My teaching is not mine, but his who sent me. —*John 7:16.*

It began with the Trinitarian formula for baptism. Later, the apostles took what Jesus had handed on to them orally and built around the Trinitarian formula

---

[10] *CCC, #175.*

the 12 articles of faith which the early Church called the *symbol*, and which later came to be called the Apostles Creed. Along with this they taught the Ten Commandments, the Seven Sacraments, and the seven petitions of the Lord's Prayer, and centered all around the real presence of Jesus in the Eucharistic Sacrifice, which they called the Lord's Supper. This was the catechetical program of the apostles and the Fathers, and it remains today the backbone of all authentic catechetical teaching.

As time went on, however, there were those who wanted to add to, subtract from or modify the Deposit of Faith to their own liking, and there developed a need for a standard, a yardstick, against which to measure a teaching to determine whether it belonged to the Deposit of Faith. St. Irenaeus was to play a substantial role in this chapter as well.

CHAPTER TWO

THE RULE OF FAITH

—∾—

Sacred Scripture, Sacred Tradition and the teaching authority of the Church (The Magisterium) together comprise what is commonly known as the *Deposit of Faith*. It is what is referred to by St. Paul in First Timothy with the admonition:

> O Timothy, guard what has been entrusted to you. Avoid the godless chatter and contradictions of what is falsely called knowledge, for by professing it some have missed the mark as regards the faith.
>
> — *1 Timothy 6:20*

But although Sacred Scripture, Sacred Tradition and the Magisterium together comprise the Deposit of Faith, it is critical to grasp the precise relationship among the three. Toward this end, we can do no better than to consult the words of the Catechism itself. This relationship is explained masterfully in paragraphs 81, 82, 85 and 86 of the Catechism, as follows:

81. *"Sacred Scripture* is the speech of God as it is put down in writing under the breath of the Holy Spirit."

And[Holy] *Tradition* transmits in its entirety the Word of God which has been entrusted to the apostles by Christ the Lord and the Holy Spirit. It transmits it to the successors of the apostles so that, enlightened by the Spirit of truth, they may faithfully preserve, expound and spread it abroad by their preaching."[11]

---

[11] *Dei Verbum #9.*

82. As a result the Church, to whom the transmission and interpretation of Revelation is entrusted, "does not derive her certainty about all revealed truths from the holy Scriptures alone. Both Scripture and Tradition must be accepted and honored with equal sentiments of devotion and reverence."[12]

85. "The task of giving an authentic interpretation of the Word of God, whether in its written form or in the form of Tradition, has been entrusted to the living, teaching office of the Church alone. Its authority in this matter is exercised in the name of Jesus Christ. This means that the task of interpretation has been entrusted to the bishops in communion with the successor of Peter, the Bishop of Rome."[13]

---

[12] *Dei Verbum, #9.*

[13] *Dei Verbum, #12, §2.*

86. "Yet this Magisterium is not superior to the Word of God, but its servant. It teaches only what has been handed on to it. At the divine command and with the help of the Holy Spirit, it listens to this devotedly, guards it with dedication, and expounds it faithfully. All that it proposes for belief as being divinely revealed is drawn from this single deposit of faith."[14]

Today, we have the benefit of two thousand years of history, during which the Magisterium has already defined many doctrines as belonging to the Deposit of Faith, and ruled out others as not belonging to the Deposit. But it still happens that scripture scholars propose new interpretations of scripture, and theologians propose interpretations of doctrine which are questionable. How do we evaluate such events? The problem is as old as the Church itself. The solution was proposed by St. Irenaeus of Lyons in his treatise

---

[14] *Dei Verbum #10, §2.*

Against Heresies, in which he gave a passionate and articulate refutation of the Gnostic heresy. The solution is called the *Rule of Faith*.

Although the *Rule of Faith* is primarily thought of as a rule for testing the interpretation of scripture, it is equally valid for testing any proposed teaching. As the Second Vatican Council taught:

> But the task of authentically interpreting the word of God, whether written or handed on, has been entrusted exclusively to the living teaching office of the Church...It is clear, therefore, that sacred tradition, Sacred Scripture and the teaching authority of the Church, in accord with God's wise design, are so linked and joined together that one cannot stand without the others, and that all together and each in its own way under the action of the one Holy Spirit contribute effectively to the salvation of souls.[15]

---

[15] *Dei Verbum, #10.*

The Greek word which is translated into English as "rule" was "canon" (κανών), which means rule in the sense of yardstick or measuring rod. This is the source of the English word "ruler." You know if something is twelve inches long by comparing it to a ruler, because you already know the ruler is twelve inches long. To the Greeks, a κανων was a standard against which something was measured. According to one scripture scholar: "to say that the books of the bible are 'canonical' is to say that they are 'normative.' For Christian faith and life: 'Canon' etymologically means 'norm.'"[16] So the *Rule of Faith* is the norm against which we measure a proposed interpretation of scripture or teaching to determine whether it is consistent with the *Deposit of Faith*.

The Catechism discusses the *Rule of Faith* in the section dealing with interpretation of scripture, paragraphs 111-114. It begins by pointing out in paragraph 111 that: "Sacred Scripture must be read and

---

[16] Joseph T. Linehard, *The Bible, The Church and Authority,* (Collegeville, Minnesota, 1995), p. 79.

interpreted in the light of the same Spirit (the Holy Spirit) by whom it is written."[17] It then sets forth in paragraphs 112-114 three key criteria for interpreting Scripture:

1. *Be especially attentive to the content and unity of the whole Scripture.*

2. *Read the Scripture within "the living tradition of the whole Church."*

3. *Be attentive to the analogy of faith.*

These three paragraphs together can be regarded as a summary of the *Rule of Faith*. In other words, the Rule of Faith is that: Scripture must be interpreted consistent with the content and unity of the whole Scripture, in accordance with the living Tradition of the whole Church, and with attention to the analogy of faith.

The *analogy of faith* in this sense is an aspect, or subset of the *Rule of Faith*. The *analogy of faith* holds

---

[17] This is a direct quote from *Dei Verbum #12*.

that truth cannot contradict itself. What this means is that a proposed interpretation of a biblical passage or a doctrine cannot be true if it contradicts another passage of scripture, or a doctrinal teaching that has been defined by the Magisterium as belonging to the Deposit of Faith.

An example of the operation of the *Rule of Faith* would be the controversy over the well-known "brethren of the Lord" passage in Mark 3:31ff. The Magisterium has formally defined the perpetual virginity of Mary as a dogma of the Church. This means that it is part of the *Deposit of Faith*, contained in Revelation and necessary for salvation. A dogma is the highest form of Church teaching. It has been definitively defined, and all of the faithful are obligated to give it the assent of faith. Concerning dogma, the Catechism teaches:

> The Church's Magisterium exercises the authority it holds from Christ to its fullest extent when it defines dogmas, that is, when

38

it proposes, in a form obliging the Christian people to an irrevocable adherence of faith, truths contained in divine Revelation or also when it proposes, in a definitive way, truths having a necessary connection with these.[18]

Some have proposed a literalist interpretation of Mark 3:31, which would mean that Jesus had siblings, i.e. Mary had other children, and therefore was not a perpetual virgin. The *Rule (analogy) of Faith* holds that two truths cannot contradict one another. The Church has defined the perpetual virginity of Mary as dogma (truth). Therefore, the Rule of Faith teaches that an interpretation of Mark 3:31ff in which the original Greek word which is translated as "brethren" means "siblings," cannot be correct. An alternative interpretation must be sought. Various alternatives have been proposed; one such is that the original Greek word can also mean "cousin" or "kinsman." Another is that the "brethren" were the

---

[18] *CCC, #88.*

sons of Joseph by a deceased first wife. It is beyond our scope here to choose among these various interpretations, but this is an example of the operation of the *Rule of Faith* as a principle of biblical interpretation. The Church has always taught that Scripture is inerrant. The Second Vatican Council, in the *Dogmatic Constitution on Divine Revelation, (Dei Verbum)*, taught:

> Therefore, since everything asserted by the inspired authors or sacred writers must be held to be asserted by the Holy Spirit, it follows that the books of Scripture must be acknowledged as teaching solidly, faithfully and without error that truth which God, for the sake of salvation, wanted put into sacred writings.[19]

Hence the *Rule of Faith* requires us to approach Scripture with the presupposition that it is inerrant,

---

[19] *Dei Verbum #11.*

and also that it is a coherent unity which tells one story, the story of God's everlasting love and saving deeds, from Genesis to Revelation. In Scripture God tells us truths which we need to know for our salvation, but he does not tell us everything at once. He has told it to us in progressive increments, and the story deepens as our capacity to receive it matures.

But the *Rule of Faith* teaches that each revealed truth must harmonize and coincide with all previous truths. In interpreting Scripture, we seek the literal meaning first. But if the literal meaning contradicts the established meaning of another passage of Scripture, or of the Word of God (Scripture and Tradition) as a whole, then we must return to the text and look to philology, literary form, analogy, allegory, and other vehicles to find a meaning that harmonizes with the unity and coherence of Scripture.

The Rule of Faith, then, is a rule of coherence, of harmonization. It requires that any proposed inter-pretation of Scripture must be consistent with the coherence of the whole of Scripture, and with Sacred Tradition as handed on by the Magisterium, and that it may not contradict any other revealed truth.

CHAPTER THREE

THE STANDARD
OF FAITH

—〜〜—

The Standard of Faith (teaching) refers to the method of handing on the faith the way Jesus and the Apostles handed it on to us. The source of this concept comes from St. Paul's Letter to the Romans:

> But thanks be to God, that you who were once slaves to sin have become obedient from the heart to the standard of teaching to which you were committed.
>
> —*Romans 6:17*[20]

---

[20] From the Revised Standard Version, Catholic Edition.

The phrase translated above by the RSV-CE as a "standard of teaching to which you were committed" is translated by the New American Bible as a "pattern of teaching to which you were entrusted." The key phrase in the original Greek is: παρεδοθητε τυπον διδαχης. At their roots, the key words are "Paradosis," which means "to had on" in the sense of oral transmission, and "tupos didache," which means "pattern of teaching," or "standard of teaching," or "standard of faith."

"Tupos didache" is the pattern of teaching which Jesus used to teach the apostles, and which they handed on to their successors, the bishops whom they appointed. From the very beginning, the teaching of the apostles and of the early Church Fathers followed this pattern of teaching. The idea was to "hand on" the Revelation, the divine truths necessary for our salvation which had been revealed by God, first in a veiled form through Moses and the prophets, and in later times through the words and deeds of Jesus Christ as he walked among us.

The words of Moses and the prophets were relevant to our salvation because they "pointed to" the Paschal Mystery—the passion, death, resurrection and ascension of Jesus. This is known as the "spiritual sense" of Scripture.

The "tupos didache" or pattern of teaching of the apostles had two main hallmarks: it was Christocentric (centered on Christ) and it was based on the Scriptures. Since the New Testament had not been written yet at the time of the apostles' initial teaching, this means that it was based on "typology" or the spiritual sense of the Old Testament Scriptures, the way in which they pointed to or pre-figured the Paschal Mystery of Jesus Christ.

The earliest example of the tupos didache that we have is found in Acts 2:14-41. It is Peter's first proclamation of the *kerygma*, the Gospel message. The time is immediately after Pentecost. Peter and the other apostles and disciples had just received a new and fresh outpouring of the Holy Spirit in special way. [21] Scripture tells us:

> And they were all filled with the Holy Spirit, and they began to speak in other tongues, as the Spirit gave them utterance.
> —*Acts 2:4*

There were diaspora Jews from all over the world in Jerusalem at that time for the festival, and they each heard and understood the apostles in their own tongues. Some of the local Jews began to mock the apostles, intimating that they must be drunk because they were speaking in tongues. Peter then embarked on his discourse, which is a classic example of the tupos didache. He taught with authority and enthusiasm. He taught by giving personal witness. These

---

[21] This was not the first time they received the Holy Spirit. Since they Apostles were ordained at the Last Supper, they must have received the Holy Spirit then. But Pentecost was a new and fresh outpouring of the gifts of the Holy Spirit upon them.

46

are also characteristics of the tupos didache. Peter's discourse is as follows:

"Men of Judea and all who dwell in Jerusalem, let this be known to you, and give ear to my words. For these men are not drunk as you suppose, since it is only the third hour of the day; but this is what was spoken through the prophet Joel:

"And in the last days it shall be, God declares,
that I will pour out my Spirit upon all flesh,
and your sons and your daughters shall prophesy,
and your young men shall see visions,
and your old men shall dream dreams;
yea, and on my menservants and my maidservants in those days
I will pour out my Spirit; and they shall prophesy.

And I will show wonders in the heavens
above
And signs on the earth beneath,
Blood, and fire, and vapor of smoke;
The sun shall be turned into darkness
And the moon into blood,
Before the day of the Lord comes,
The great and manifest day.
And it shall be that whoever calls upon the
name of the Lord shall be saved."

Men of Israel, hear these words: Jesus of
Nazareth, a man attested to you by God with
mighty works and wonders and signs which
God did through him in your midst, as you
yourselves know—this Jesus, delivered up
according to the definite plan and foreknowl-
edge of God, you crucified and killed by the
hands of lawless men. But God raised him
up, having loosed the pangs of death, for it

48

was not possible for him to be held by it. For David says concerning him:

"I saw the Lord always before me,

for he is at my right hand that I may not be shaken;

therefore my heart was glad, and my tongue rejoiced;

moreover my flesh will dwell in hope.

For thou wilt not abandon my soul to Hades,

Nor let the Holy One see corruption.

Thou hast made known to me the ways of life;

Thou wilt make me full of gladness with thy presence."

Brethren, I may say confidently of the Patriarch David that he both died and was buried, and his tomb is with us to this day. Being therefore a prophet and knowing that God had sworn an oath to him that he would set one of his descendants on his throne, he foresaw and spoke of the resurrection of the Christ, that he was not abandoned to Hades, nor did his flesh see corruption. This Jesus God raised up and of that we are all witnesses. Being therefore exalted at the right hand of God, and having received from the Father the promise of the Holy Spirit, he has poured out this which you see and hear. For David did not ascend into the heavens, but he himself says,

"The Lord said to my Lord, sit at my right hand, till I make thy enemies a footstool for thy feet."

Let all the house of Israel therefore know assuredly that God has made him both Lord and Christ, this Jesus whom you crucified."

Now when they heard this they were cut to the heart, and said to Peter and the rest of the Apostles, "Brethren, what shall we do?" And Peter said to them, "Repent and be baptized every one of you in the name of Jesus Christ for the forgiveness of your sins, and you shall receive the gift of the Holy Spirit. For the promise is to you and to your children and to all who are far off, every one of whom the Lord calls to him. And he testified with many other words and exhorted them, saying, "Save yourselves from this crooked generation." So those who received his words were baptized and there were added that day about three thousand souls.

—*Acts 2:14-41.*

This is the first proclamation of what came to be known as the *"kerygma,"* the proclamation of the Gospel message, the good news of salvation through the incarnation, passion, death, resurrection and ascension of Jesus Christ. It has all of the character-istics of what later came to be known as the *tupos didache* or standard of teaching of the apostles. For example:

- It is **Trinitarian.** ("*Being therefore exalted at the right hand of God, and having received from the Father the promise of the Holy Spirit, he has poured out this which you see and hear.*")

- It is **Christocentric**. This entire discourse centers around the saving words and deeds of Jesus Christ, and how all things in the Hebrew Scriptures point to him.

- It is **Scriptural.** This relatively short discourse contains at least eight quotes from or refer-ences to the Old Testament scriptures: Joel 2:22-38; Psalm 69:25; Psalm 109:8; Psalm 16:8-11; Psalm 132:11; Psalm 16:10; Psalm 110:1; and Isaiah 57:19. Peter's purpose in using all of these quotes and references was to show that the Paschal Mystery of Jesus

Christ is the fulfillment of all that was prophesied in the Old Testament. This is known as the *spiritual sense* of scripture.

It is a personal **witness**, a testimony. Peter is giving his personal witness to what he has seen and heard, to the saving power of the deeds and words of Jesus Christ, and the power of the Holy Spirit, the *paraclete,* who proceeds from the Father and the Son. The apostles and the Fathers never just taught facts or doctrines, they gave personal witness to the power of Jesus Christ in their lives. They did this by telling the story of salvation history.

Peter's personal witness required and received a **response**. The first question Peter was asked after he finished the story was: "Brothers, what shall we do?" Peter answered them: "Repent and be baptized every one of you in the name of Jesus Christ for the forgiveness of your sins; and you shall receive the gift of the Holy Spirit."

This is the *tupos didache*. This is the standard of teaching of the apostles. They always did it this way. Their teaching was always **Trinitarian**, **Christocentric**, **Scriptural**, it was done through **personal witness**, and it provoked a **response** in all those who opened themselves to God's grace and the power of the Holy Spirit.

What was the response? In the case of Peter's *kerygma*, Acts 2:41 tells us they repented and 3,000 were baptized that day! And then what did they do? Acts 2:42 tells us:

And they devoted themselves to the apostles' teaching and fellowship, to the breaking of the bread and the prayers.

This verse from the Acts of the Apostles is extremely important for all catechists. It is a shorthand description of the structure of the Catechumenate from Apostolic times down to the present day. It is the same pattern of spiritual life that was used in the Jewish synagogue.

The phrases contained in acts 2:42 describe the four phases of the catechumenate, the four pillars of the Church, (one, holy, Catholic and apostolic), and the four parts of the Catechism of the Catholic Church. The connection can be seen as follows:

They devoted themselves to:

Acts 2:42	Catechism
The Teaching of the Apostles	Creed (Part I)
The Fellowship	Life in Christ (Part 3)
The Breaking of the Bread	The Sacraments (Part 2)
The Prayers	The Prayers (Part 4)

By "the Teaching of the Apostles," *Acts* is referring to both the Deposit of Faith and the Standard of Faith, i.e. the *paratheke* and the *tupos didache*; the content that was taught and the way it was taught.

This consisted of the twelve articles of the Creed, the Ten Commandments, the seven sacraments and the seven petitions of the Lord's Prayer.

By the word "fellowship," Acts is describing the entire moral life of the Christian community. This is further described in Acts 4:32:

> Now the company of those who believed were of one heart and soul, and no one said that any of the things that he possessed was his own, but they had everything in common.

By the phrase "breaking of the bread," Acts is referring to the liturgy and the sacramental life, especially the Eucharist. From the very earliest times, the Christian community gathered on the first day of the week to celebrate the Lord's Supper—the breaking of the bread. It is important for the catechist not to get bogged down in the question which has distracted and side-tracked some contemporary theologians—the question of when the Church first taught dogmatically that there are seven sacraments. It doesn't matter for purposes of catechesis. What does matter is that all of the sacraments were present in the early Church, all of them were instituted by Christ and were based in Scripture,[22] and together they constituted the sacramental life, the *Deposit of Grace*, which Acts 2:42 refers to as "the breaking of the bread."

Finally, we have the prayers. The Catechism defines prayer as "the living relationship of the children of God with the Father who is good beyond measure, with his Son Jesus Christ, and with the Holy Spirit. The grace of the kingdom is the union of the entire holy and royal Trinity...with the whole human spirit."[23]

The apostles and their successors primarily used the Our Father both to teach prayer and to teach doctrine. The Our Father is, in a sense, a concise summary of the faith. It is the perfect prayer, and the

---

[22] *CCC #1114, 1210.*

[23] *CCC, #2565.*

only prayer that Jesus himself taught us. It contains seven petitions—no accident, because in Jewish thought, the number seven represent fullness, perfection, and covenant.

The Our Father contains seven petitions. The first three draw us toward the Father: *thy name, thy will, thy kingdom*;[24] the fourth and fifth petitions concern our life as such, to be fed and to be healed of sin,[25] and the sixth and seventh petitions concern our battle for victory over sin.

All those who exercise a share in the teaching office of the Church by delegation from the bishop, who is the primary teacher in each diocese, have a solemn duty. Our duty is to teach what Jesus taught the apostles and they handed down to us through their successors (Deposit of Faith), which has been tested and confirmed by the Rule of Faith, and to teach it the way the apostles taught it (Standard of Faith). We do not teach our own opinions, or the

---

[24] *CCC, #2804.*

[25] *CCC, #2805.*

opinions and theories of theologians. Nor do we ask those whom we are entrusted to teach for their opinions. The *Deposit of Faith* is not a matter of opinion, but of truth—revealed by God, for the sake of our salvation.[26] Our obligation is to teach what has been handed on to us—with the mind of the Church, from the heart of the Church.

---

[26] Cf. Dei Verbum, #11.

CHAPTER FOUR

THE DEPOSIT OF GRACE

—∿—

G race is a participation in the life of God.[27] It is the divine help which God gives us to enable us to do good and avoid evil, and to come to know him, love him and serve him. Grace comes to us as a gratuitous gift from God. We do not deserve it, and we cannot earn it. And God does not force it on us. We can and must freely choose to accept it and cooperate with it.

The *Deposit of Grace* is God's life entrusted to the Church, through the apostles and their successors, so that through the working of the Holy Spirit, everyone may enter into adopted sonship with God. Just before his ascension, Jesus commissioned the

---

[27] *CCC, #1997.*

apostles to commission others to hand on the Deposit of Grace, saying:

> All authority in heaven and on earth has been given to me. Go therefore and make disciples of all nations, baptizing them in the name of the Father and of the Son and of the Holy Spirit,[28] teaching them to observe all that I have commanded you;[29] and behold I am with you always, to the close of the age.
> —*Matthew 28:18-20.*

The Pope and the bishops today can trace their ordination through an unbroken line of succession to the apostles themselves. This is called "apostolic succession." In the Creed, we profess our belief in what are called the four marks of the Church: "One, Holy, Catholic and Apostolic." Thus, the succession of the bishops through an unbroken chain of ordina-

---

[28] *Deposit of Grace.*

[29] *Deposit of Faith.*

tion from the apostles themselves is the proof that the Church is apostolic, and it is the source of the Church's authority to guard and dispense the *Deposit of Grace*. The bishops are the visible representatives of Christ himself through the apostles, and the Holy Spirit works through them and guides and protects them. The Catechism teaches that "grace is first and foremost the gift of the Spirit who justifies and sanctifies us."[30]

The obligation of the catechist is to teach the *Deposit of Faith* and the *Deposit of Grace* as twin channels of God's gift to his people who are united by the bond of faith in a share in the divine life of the Trinity. Through the *Deposit of Faith* we can know the truths which God has revealed for the sake of our salvation, and through the *Deposit of Grace* we are strengthened and empowered to live in communion with the Trinity.

There are two kinds of grace. *Sanctifying grace* is the gratuitous gift that God gives us of his own life,

---

[30] *CCC, #2003.*

infused into our soul to heal us and sanctify us. It is also known as habitual grace.[31] *Actual grace* is God's intervention, whether at the beginning of conversion or in the course of our faith journey, which enables us to do good and avoid evil.[32]

The specific way that the Church delivers the *Deposit of Grace* is through the sacraments. The old *Baltimore Catechism* defined the sacraments as "outward signs instituted by Christ to give grace," and so they are.

The word *sacrament* comes from the Latin word *sacramentum*, which means oath. But it meant a particular type of oath. It was the oath that a soldier swore when he entered the Army. By this oath he entered into a covenant relationship with his fellow soldiers, with his Centurions, Generals and ultimately with the Emperor. He exchanged the white tunic of a citizen for the red tunic of a Legionnaire, and he took on a new sign and a symbol that he was willing

---

[31] *CCC, #1999.*

[32] *CCC, #2000.*

to die for his brothers in arms, and they were willing to die for him.

A covenant is more than a contract; it unites the parties in a bond of sacred kinship. In Hebrew as well, the word for *oath* was the same as the word for *Covenant*, and it came from the same root as the word for *seven,* so that in a literal sense, in Hebrew to swear an oath was to *seven oneself.*[33]

All of the sacraments are part of the Deposit of Grace, but we can see this in a special way in the Sacraments of Baptism and Eucharist.

Jesus allowed himself to be baptized, in order to set an example for us, to show us how we are to enter into the divine life of the Trinity. Matthew tells us:

Then Jesus came from Galilee to the Jordan to John, to be baptized by him. John would have prevented him, saying, "I need to be baptized by you, and do you come to me?" But Jesus

---

[33] Scott Hahn, Ph.D., *Understanding the Scriptures,* (Woodridge, Illinois, 2005), p. 49.

answered him, "Let it be so now; for thus it is fitting for us to fulfill all righteousness." Then he consented. And when Jesus was baptized, he went up immediately from the water, and behold, the heavens were opened and he saw the Spirit of God descending like a dove, and alighting on him; and behold, a voice from heaven, saying, "This is my beloved Son, with whom I am well pleased."

Matthew 3:13-17.

The same passage is found in Mark 1:9-11; Luke 3:21-22; and John 1:31-34. All four evangelists considered it important enough to set forth at the beginning of their account of Jesus life and ministry. Through it, the Holy Spirit instructs us that we are to access the Deposit of Grace through the Sacrament of Baptism. Jesus said to Nicodemus:

Amen, Amen I say to you, no one can enter the kingdom of God without being born of water and the Spirit.

John 3:5.

Likewise, Jesus instituted the Eucharist at the Last Supper. In St. Matthew's account we are told:

Now as they were eating, Jesus took bread and blessed and broke it, and gave it to the disciples and said, "Take, eat, this is my body." "And he took a chalice, and when he had given thanks he gave it to them, saying, "Drink of it, all of you, for this is my blood of the covenant, which is poured out for many for the forgiveness of sins. I tell you I shall not drink again of the fruit of the vine until the day when I drink it anew in my Father's kingdom."

—*Matthew 26:26-29.*

The same account is found in Mark 14:22ff, Luke 22:17ff, and 1 Corinthians 11:23-26. The Church has always considered these passages, which are all accounts of the same event, to be the institution texts of the Sacrament of the Eucharist. The Second Vatican Council called the Eucharist "the source and summit of the Christian life."[34]

Baptism and the Eucharist are the keys, in a sense the portals to the *Deposit of Grace*, but all of the sacraments are part of the *Deposit of Grace*, because all were instituted by Christ, entrusted to the apostles and their successors, and all are sources of sanctifying grace for the Church and all of her members. All of the sacraments are based on institution texts in Sacred Scripture.

This is the way they are to be taught by the catechist. In recent years, some catechetical texts have become sidetracked into discussion of whether there could have been more or less than seven sacraments, or when the sacraments were formally dogmatically

---

[34] *Lumen Gentium #11, CCC #1324.*

proclaimed, etc. There may be a place in the seminary or graduate school classroom for such theoretical speculation, but it is never appropriate in the catechumenate. The sacred duty of the catechist is to hand on the Deposit of Faith and the Deposit of Grace as Jesus handed it on to the apostles, and as it is found in both Sacred Scripture and the Tradition of the Church.

CHAPTER FIVE

THE FORTY DAYS

—⟋⟍—

The forty days from the Resurrection to the Ascension are extremely important to the catechist, and their importance is very rarely taught or even discussed in seminaries or religious studies programs. In a very real sense, the forty days was the seminary of the apostles. It was during these forty days that Jesus explained to the apostles the significance and meaning of his words and deeds during his public ministry. During these forty days, Jesus taught the apostles how and what to teach, he rehabilitated them, and he gave them *peace* and *hope*.

This was, in a sense, the apostles' *Mystagogia*. Mystagogia means going deeper in what you already have. In apostolic times, the apostles catechized the catechumens by teaching them the Creed, the Ten Commandments, the seven petitions of the Our Father and the Seven Sacraments. They required the catechumens to live a moral Christian life and to study those three elements of the Trinitarian faith for approximately three years. Then, if the community and the Bishop judged them ready, they were baptized, confirmed and received their First Eucharist all at the same time, at the Easter Vigil. Then, after their baptism, there came a period of *Mystagogia* in which the apostles explained the meaning of the sacraments to them. It was the belief of the early Church that the catechumens needed the grace of the sacraments before they could understand them. So they gave them the sacraments first, and then, in a post-baptismal period of living a life of grace, they explained the meaning of the sacred mysteries to them.

Jesus had two plans. One was for us, and one was for the devil. His plan for us was to get to us through the teaching of the apostles. Jesus never wrote any books. He never wrote any letters. His entire plan was to tell the apostles those truths which are necessary for salvation, and to authorize them to appoint successors and to hand those truths down to us through those successors. The words catechesis, catechist and catechism all come from the Greek word *"catechein,"* which means "to echo down."

His plan for the devil was to vanquish him. When he went into the desert after his baptism in the Jordan by John, he encountered the devil and the devil tempted him, but he resisted every temptation and the devil was defeated. This story is given in essentially the same form by all three synoptic Gospels.[35] Matthew and Mark both tell us that after Jesus defeated the temptations of the devil, "angels came and ministered to him."

There are six scripture passages which are essential to understanding the significance of the apostles' seminary formation during the Forty Days. But prior to that, we need to take a look at the significance of Matthew 13:10-17. This important scripture passage

---

[35] *Matthew 4:1-11; Mark 1:12-13; Luke 4:1-13.*

is not part of the Forty Days—it relates an incident which took place significantly prior to the Forty Days, but it is essential to the creation of a framework for understanding and interpreting the Forty Days. Matthew tells us:

Then the disciples came and said to him, "Why do you speak to them in parables?" And he answered them, "To you it has been given to know the secrets of the kingdom of heaven, but to them it has not been given. For to him who has more will be given, and he will have abundance; but from him who has not, even what he has will be taken away. This is why I speak to them in parables, because seeing they do not see, and hearing they do not hear, nor do they understand. With them indeed is fulfilled the prophecy of Isaiah which says:

You shall indeed hear but never understand,
And you shall indeed see but never perceive.

For this people's heart has grown dull,

And their ears are heavy of hearing,

And their eyes they have closed,

Lest they should perceive with their eyes,

And hear with their ears,

And understand with their heart,

And turn to me to heal them.

But blessed are your eyes, for they see, and your ears, for they hear. Truly, I say to you, many prophets and righteous men longed to see what you see, and did not see it, and to hear what you hear, and did not hear it.

This passage is critical, because it is the conception of the Church, and the preview of the Forty Days. Undoubtedly you have heard many homilies on Pentecost Sunday to the effect that Pentecost was the "birthday of the Church." And so it was, in the sense that it was the day on which the Church was first made manifest to the world. But it was not the day on which the Church was first conceived. The Church was conceived back in Matthew 13:10, when Jesus said to the apostles: "To you it has been given to know the secrets of the kingdom of heaven..." In essence, Jesus is saying to the apostles here: "You will be the *Magisterium*, the teaching office. You will decide what is sound doctrine and what is not. You will receive the *Mystagogia*, and you will pass it on."

The content of the Mystagogia which the apostles received during the Forty Days can be seen in the following six key passages:

The Road to Emmaus

That very day two of them were going to a village named Emmaus, about seven miles from Jerusalem, and talking with each other about these things which had happened. While they were talking and discussing together, Jesus himself drew near and went with them. But their eyes were kept from recognizing him. And he said to them, "What

76

is this conversation you are holding with each other as you walk?" And they stood still, looking sad. Then one of them, named Cleopas, answered him, "Are you the only visitor to Jerusalem who does not know the things that have happened there in these days?" And he said to them, "What things?" And they said to him, "Concerning Jesus of Nazareth, who was a prophet mighty in deed and word before God and all the people, and how our chief priests and rulers delivered him up to be condemned to death, and crucified him. But we had hoped that he was the one to redeem Israel. Yes, and besides all this, it is now the third day since this happened. Moreover, some women of our company amazed us. They were at the tomb early in the morning and did not find his body; and they came back saying that they had seen a vision of angels, who said that he was alive. Some of those who were with us went to the tomb, and found it just as the women had said; but him they did not see." And he said to them, "O foolish men, and slow of heart to believe all that the prophets have spoken! Was it not necessary that Christ should suffer these things and enter into his glory?" And beginning with Moses and all the prophets, he interpreted to them in all the Scriptures the things concerning himself.

So they drew near to the village to which they were going. He appeared to be going further, but they constrained him, saying, "Stay with us, for it is toward evening and the day is now far spent." So he went in to stay with them. When he was at table with them, he took the bread and blessed and broke it, and gave it to them. And their eyes were opened and they recognized him; and he vanished out of their sight. They said to each other, "Did not our hearts burn within us while he talked to us on the road, while he opened to us the Scriptures?" And they rose that same hour and returned to Jerusalem; and they found the Eleven gathered together and those who were with them, who said, "The Lord has risen indeed and has appeared to Simon!" Then they told what happened on the road, and how he was known to them in the breaking of the bread.

This is the famous passage of the encounter on the Road to Emmaus. Most people are aware that this passage is connected to the Eucharist, and that the fact that the disciples recognized Jesus in the breaking of the bread is a figure for the Eucharist. This is correct, but there is much more to the catechetical significance of this passage.

The disciples initially do not recognize Jesus, and he begins to break open the Scriptures for them. "Beginning with Moses and the prophets, he interpreted for them all in the Scriptures concerning him." We see here the "Principle of Fulfillment" — how Jesus fulfilled all that was prophesied in the Old Testament, and all of the typology contained in the Old Testament. In other words, Adam, Noah, Abraham, Isaac, Joseph, Moses, and David were all "types" of Jesus; that is they all foreshadowed in some way what would be fully made manifest in Jesus.[36]

We see here also the structure of the Mass. Jesus first broke open the Scriptures for them; that is, he called to mind the Old Testament Scriptures that they were familiar with, and then he explained how they related to him. Then he broke bread with them, "and they recognized him in the breaking of the bread." This is the structure of the Mass. First we have the breaking open of the Scriptures (the Liturgy of the Word), then we have the homily, explaining the Scriptures and how they relate to the Paschal Mystery, and then we have the "breaking of the bread" (Liturgy of the Eucharist.) The breaking of the bread never precedes the breaking open of the Scriptures, but always follows it.

---

[36] *CCC, #128-130.*

Jesus is rehabilitating the apostles during this period. They need to be rehabilitated because during the Passion they all—except John—ran and hid out of fear. He is also teaching them the content of the catechesis they are to hand on, and giving them a lesson in the theological virtue of hope. The next critical Scripture passage for an understand of The Forty Days is *John 20:19-23*:

On the evening of that day, the first day of the week, the doors being shut where the disciples were, for fear of the Jews, Jesus came and stood among them and said to them, "Peace be with you." When he had said this, he showed them his hands and his side. Then the disciples were glad when they saw the Lord. Jesus said to them again, "Peace be with you. As the Father has sent me, even so I send you." And when he had said this, he breathed on them, and said to them, "Receive the Holy Spirit. If you forgive the sins of any,

they are forgiven; if you retain the sins of any,
they are retained."

In this passage, we have the institution of the Sacrament of Reconciliation. Many people incorrectly think that Matthew 16:18-20 was the institution of the Sacrament of Reconciliation, but it was not. That was the institution of the primacy of Peter. The Sacrament of Reconciliation could not have been instituted until after Jesus atoned for our sins on the Cross. Jesus instituted the Sacrament of Reconciliation when he appeared to the apostles after the Resurrection, recorded in John 20:19-23, cited above.

We also see in this passage that Jesus gives the apostles *peace*. This is very important. In order to get *hope*, they need to get *peace*. The theological virtue of hope allows us to "place our trust in Christ's promises relying not on our own strength, but on the help and grace of the Holy Spirit."[37] By giving them

---

[37] *CCC, #1817.*

peace, Jesus is giving them the grace that restores their hope.

The next Scripture passage which gives us a glimpse of The Forty Days is John 20:24-29:

Now Thomas, one of the Twelve, called the Twin, was not with them when Jesus came. So the other disciples told him "We have seen the Lord."" But he said to them, "Unless I see in his hands the print of the nails, and place my finger in the mark of the nails, and place my hand in his side, I will not believe."

Eight days later, his disciples were again in the house, and Thomas was with them. The doors were shut, but Jesus came and stood among them and said, "Peace be with you." Then he said to Thomas, "Put your finger here, and see my hands; and put out your hand, and place it in my side; do not be faithless, but believing." Thomas answered him, "My Lord and my God!" Jesus said to him,

"You have believed because you have seen me. Blessed are those who have not seen and yet believe."

Virtually everyone is familiar with this passage. It is called the story of "Doubting Thomas." But we shouldn't call him "Doubting Thomas," because actually all the apostles doubted. In fact, as we shall see shortly, some of them were still doubting as they watched Jesus ascend into heaven before their eyes. In fact, the important thing about this passage is not Thomas' doubt, but his confession of faith: "My Lord and my God." It is also important in this passage that Jesus tells the disciple that others will believe without seeing what they have seen. In other words, others will believe on the strength of the apostles' testimony. This is all part of the rehabilitation of the apostles, and the formation of the apostles as bishops, catechists and preachers.

The next passage in the apostles seminary is John 21:15-19:

When they had finished breakfast, Jesus said to Simon Peter, "Simon, son of John, do you love me more than these?" He said to him, "Yes, Lord; you know that I love you." He said to him, "Feed my lambs." A second time he said to him, "Simon, son of John, do you love me?" He said to him, "Yes, Lord; you know that I love you." He said to him, "Tend my sheep." He said to him the third time, "Simon, son of John, do you love me?" Peter was grieved because he said to him the third time, "Do you love me?" And he said to him, "Lord, you know everything; you know that I love you." Jesus said to him, "Feed my sheep." "Truly, truly, I say too you, when you were young, you fastened your own belt and walked where you would; but when you are old, you will stretch out your hands, and another will fasten your belt for you and carry you where you do not wish to go." (This he said to show by what death he was to glorify God.) And after this he said to him, "Follow me."

This passage shows, of course, the rehabilitation of Peter from denying Jesus three times on the night of His Passion. Peter is rehabilitated in the sight of the other apostles, and this is very important so that he could have primacy over them. It is important not only because Peter had to know that he was forgiven, but because the other apostles needed to see that Jesus had restored him to his role of primacy.

In the culture of the times the shepherd was an authority figure. The sheep knew the shepherd's voice and obeyed him. The shepherd completely cared for the sheep, and he had authority over them. Thus, the role of feeding and tending the sheep is an authority role. This passage signified the rehabilitation of Peter, but it signifies more. It conveys the juridical power over the Church to Peter, and through him, to the other apostles. Jesus is making Peter, and by extension the other apostles, Shepherds of Christ.

The fifth Scripture passage that is important for our understanding of The Forty Days is one of the most familiar in the Bible. It is Matthew 28:16-20:

> Now the eleven disciples went to Galilee, to the mountain to which Jesus had directed them. And when they saw him they worshiped him; but some doubted. And Jesus came and said to them, "All authority in heaven and on earth has been given to me. Go therefore and make disciples of all nations, baptizing them in the name of the Father and of the Son and of the Holy Spirit, teaching them to observe all that I have commanded you; and behold, I am with you always, to the close of the age."

This is what is commonly known as the "Great Commission." Note that, even here, "some doubted." Jesus commissions the apostles to evangelize ("Go therefore and make disciples of all nations...") and to catechize ("teaching them to observe all that I have commanded you…"). But it's more than that. Jesus tells them to baptize, and he gives them the Trinitarian formula. They had known baptism, but it was the baptism of repentance.[38] This is the only place in Scripture where we have a record of Jesus giving the apostles the Trinitarian formula of baptism. And the Trinitarian formula is accompanied by a three-fold commission: to baptize, to evangelize and to catechize. We will see later that all of the catecheses of the apostles were Trinitarian.

The final Scripture passage which is essential to an understanding of The Forty Days is Acts 1:6-14:

> So when they had come together, they asked him, "Lord, will you at this time restore the kingdom to Israel?" He said to them, "It is not for you to know times or seasons which the Father has fixed by his own authority. But you shall receive power when the Holy Spirit has come upon you; and you shall be

---

[38] Cf. *John 3:26.*

my witnesses in Jerusalem and in all Judea and Samaria and to the end of the earth. And when he had said this, as they were looking on, he was lifted up, and a cloud took him out of their sight. And while they were gazing into heaven as he went, behold, two men stood by them in white robes, and said, "Men of Galilee, why do you stand looking into heaven? This Jesus, who was taken up from you into heaven, will come in the same way as you saw him go into heaven."

This is the Ascension. It is the culmination of *The Forty Days*. It is also the culmination of the Paschal Mystery—the fulfillment of all of the typology of the Old Testament. Jesus tells the apostles where to go and how to evangelize—first to Jerusalem, then to all Judea and Samaria, and then to the ends of the earth. First to the Jews (Judea), then to the Ten Lost Tribes of Israel (Samaria), and then to the Gentiles. This is exactly what they did and how they did it as recorded in Acts Chapters 7, 8 and 9.

Note that not all authority of the Father was given to them; only the authority that had been given to Jesus. Note also that they had angels helping them. Almost everybody misses the importance of the angels in the Acts of the Apostles, but if you read the book carefully looking for them you will be astounded how many times the apostles have angels helping them.

We must also note that they did not go home. They had been rehabilitated. They stayed in Jerusalem as Jesus commanded, met in the Upper Room with Mary and the other disciples, and prayed—waiting for the Holy Spirit whom Jesus had promised to send.

The Forty Days is the apostles' Mystagogia. He depended on them to get to us. There was no "Plan B." He handed on orally to the apostles everything that we need to know for the sake of our salvation. He depended on them to get to us—and it was fulfilled.

CHAPTER SIX

THE IMPORTANCE OF THE STORY

———ᴍ———

One of the most important and effective tools in the catechist's tool box is the telling of *"The Story."* *The Story* is the story of Salvation History. It is the story of God's never-ending love. It is the story of God's intervention in human history. It is the story of God's plan of salvation. It is our story.

The *General Directory for Catechesis* particularly stresses the importance of the "presentation of salvation history by means of a biblical catechesis so as to make known the 'deeds and the words' by which God revealed himself to man..."[39]

---

[39] *GDC, #108; cf. #128, 129.*

It is important for every catechist to know how to tell the story in his or her own words. The catechist should be able to tell the story to different audiences, and to tailor it to each situation. You should be able to tell the story, as the saying goes, "at the drop of a hat." You should have in your repertoire a half-hour version of the story, a 45-minute version of the story, a sixty-minute version of the story, and so on.

Each time you tell the story, you should have in mind a general "theme." The theme can vary with the audience. For example, if you are telling the story to a group of catechists, the theme might be "truth." If you are telling it to a group of children or high school students, the theme might be "God's never-ending love." If you are telling it to a group of theology students, the theme might be "covenant." If you are telling it to a group of adults, the theme might be "faithfulness."

Today, many catechists who received degrees in Religious Studies programs have sadly never heard of the importance of telling *The Story*. The same is true for priests, deacons and seminarians. We have been taught psychological and sociological theories about teaching. We have been taught to teach students to learn from their own experiences. We have been taught to allow them to express their own opinions about God. But most of us have not been taught to tell them the story of Salvation History—of God's never-ending love.

And yet, the handing on of *The Story* is the way the apostles and Church Fathers taught. The early Church had a special name for this. It was called the *kerygma;* the initial proclamation of the Good News. This is what St. Peter was doing in Acts 2:14-36. It's what St. Stephen was doing in Acts 7, and what St. Philip was doing with the Ethiopian Eunuch in Acts 8. It is also the method of catechesis advocated by St. Augustine in his *First Catechetical Instruction.*[40]

It is still one of the most effective ways to teach the faith. The reason is simple. We are made in

---

[40] *St. Augustine, The First Catechetical Instruction,* trans. By Rev. Joseph P. Christopher, (New York, 1946), p. 18.

God's image, and God is a community of persons. Therefore we are made to be *in communio*. We are made individually, but we are not made to be isolated individually. We are made to be in a family. We have, imprinted on our soul, as it were, a desire to be in family, and to know how we fit in the family—our own family, our culture, our nation, our race, and the whole human family.

All men and women seek the answers to certain fundamental questions: Who am I? Where did I come from? Why am I here? Where am I going? How shall I live my life? What comes after this? Philosophy is nothing more than the attempt to answer these questions through human reason. Theology is the attempt to discover the answer to these questions through God's revelation.

Today, large portions of mankind, particularly in the developed world, have lost their sense of "story." We have made a god of the individual, and we have lost our sense of belonging to God's family, and of having a place and a role in God's plan. And yet, at some level we sense the loss, even if we can't express it explicitly. We long for a sense of belonging to a larger unity, of being family, of having a role in history. This is why *Roots* was such an enormously popular book and movie. This is why genealogy services make a fortune selling their services on the internet. We all want to know where we come from, whether there is a plan, and how we fit into it.

We have the answer to these questions, and we should not be timid about sharing it, not as one possible answer among many, but as **the** answer, whose author is God himself.

The Story is drawn from Scripture and the Tradition of the Church. Scripture should be used liberally in telling the story. It is a good idea to plan certain Scripture passages to illustrate certain key events in the Story, and to have certain people in the audience, especially if the audience is students, prepared to read those Scripture passages when that point in the story is reached.

The catechist should tailor the telling of the Story to his or her particular style and competence. The catechist is not just telling the story; he is testifying to its truth. You should be prepared to give examples of how God has worked in your own life to illustrate points in the story.

The question often arises as to what are the parameters of the Story. There is no hard and fast rule. The Story is God's story, and God has no beginning or end, so in a sense The Story has no beginning or end. However since you may be telling the Story in a fifty-minute class period, you had better have a beginning and an end. Many theologians would say the Story of Salvation History is from the fall of Adam to the Ascension. However, many catechists like to begin with Creation, and continue beyond the Ascension to include the Acts of the Apostles, and some even continue into the present day, include the lives of some of the key saints. Any of these approaches is acceptable.

People love stories. People learn from stories. People yearn to see how they fit into a story. All effective teachers use stories to illustrate their message, whether they realize they are doing it or not. The Story is particularly effective in catechesis, because our relationship with God is a story—the story of God's never-ending love. The outline of the story is: God created us, God loves us, God has a plan for our life, and God wants us to be in relationship with him for eternity. The duty of the catechist is to tell the Story, but not merely tell it: testify to it. Witness to its power in your own life.

CHAPTER SEVEN

THE STORY

—∿—

This is probably the only story that has no beginning and no end, because it is the story of God's never-ending love, and God has no beginning and no end.

There are two things that we need to know about God. The first is that God is transcendent. This means that he is outside of time and space. He is higher than the highest thing that we can imagine. He is love. He is goodness. He is wisdom. He cannot be limited or circumscribed in any way.

The second thing we must know about God is that he is a "Community of Persons." We use the male pronoun when speaking of Him because God has chosen to reveal himself to us as Father. But God is a Trinity: Father, Son and Holy Spirit, living in eternal, self-giving, mutual love for all eternity. The Son is the Word of God through whom all things were created. The Holy Spirit is the mutual love between the Father and the Son which overflows and pours into our souls, empowering us to do all good things.

God created the entire universe and all that is in it out of nothing. He spoke a Word. The word was the Son, the second person of the Blessed Trinity. The Creed tells us that through the Son, the Word, was created all that is. The Word of God is living and active. It does not describe, like a human word. It creates, it causes.

God created spiritual beings called angels. Angels have no bodies. They are spirits. They are pure intellect. They are more intelligent than us, so when they make a choice, they are stuck with it for all eternity. Some of the angels chose to reject God, to refuse to serve him. They are called demons, and they are followers of Lucifer, the prince of demons. They were expelled from heaven, and they wander through the world seeking the ruin of human souls. But their permanent home is Hell—the eternal abyss, where they will be consumed by their own hatred for all eternity. But there were good angels, led my Michael, the Archangel, who chose to serve God, and God assigns them to help us do good and avoid evil. They do not have bodies but occasionally in human history, at significant moments, God has sent an angel to appear in human form to help us or bring us a message.

God didn't need to create us; the Father, Son and Holy Spirit could have lived in mutual love for all eternity. But God freely chose to create the first man and the first woman in his own image and likeness. Our first parents—Adam and Eve—were created to live forever, but they chose to disobey God, and to try to become gods themselves, to decide for themselves what was good and what was evil.

Through their initial disobedience, called **original sin**, they lost paradise, and pain, sickness and death entered the world. The devil, in the form of a serpent, tempted them, but he did not make them do it. Adam and Eve made a free choice to disobey God, and as a result sin and death entered the world.

But God made a covenant with them. A covenant is more than a contract. It is a familial relationship. A contract says: I will do this if you do that. But a covenant says: I will be yours and you will be mine. When we make a covenant with someone, we enter their family, and they enter ours. Adam and Eve lost Paradise through their sin, but God promised to send a redeemer to atone for their sin and restore the promise of eternal life. A perfect synopsis of this promise is contained in Genesis 3:15, often called the *Protoevangelium*, or seed of the Gospel. God, speaking to Satan, says:

I will put enmity between you and the woman,
And between your seed and her seed;
He shall bruise your head,
And you shall bruise his heel.

This is a foreshadowing of the Incarnation and the Paschal Mystery. The woman spoken of here is Mary and her seed is Jesus, "the Christ." This is why Mary is always spoken of by the Church as "the New Eve." This was God's first covenant with man. Throughout Salvation History, man would repeatedly break the covenant, and God would repeatedly renew it. All in all, God would make five covenants with his chosen people prior to the Incarnation, when God himself would take on human flesh and enter the world.

Adam and Eve married and had children, but of their first two children, one killed the other out of jealousy. Eventually they had more children, and their descendants populated the earth. But man and woman continued to sin through all kinds of abominable acts, and eventually God decided to chastise the earth through a flood.

But God found one just man named Noah, and he decided to spare the earth. He told Noah to build an ark and take his wife and three sons and their wives, and enough animals to repopulate the earth, and put them on the ark. It rained for forty days and forty nights and the whole earth was flooded, but Noah and his family were saved. Afterwards, God told Noah to "be fruitful and multiply, and fill the earth." God made a covenant with Noah. This was the Second Covenant. He promised that he would never destroy the earth by water again, and he put a rainbow in the sky as a sign of his covenant.

Time went on and mankind multiplied, but they did not know God. There came a time when God spoke his Word to a righteous man named Abram, in Haran, which is in modern-day Iraq. God told Abram, who was already an old man, to take his tribe and his animals and go to the land of Canaan. This was a fearsome journey, on foot across many hundreds of miles, but Abram had faith, and he obeyed, along with his wife and his kinsmen.

Through many tribulations God led Abram to Canaan, which was a land rich in fruits and plants, a land which the Bible calls a land "of milk and honey." Abram settled in Canaan with his tribe, and was prosperous. But he and his elderly wife, Sarai, were childless. This was very bad at that time, because a man passed on his name and his memory through his children, especially sons.

God sent an angel to Abram and promised him a son. Sarai doubted, in fact she laughed when she heard the prophecy, but it was fulfilled, and in their old age, Sarai, whose name God changed to Sarah, gave birth to a son, who was named Isaac, which means "laughter." God changed Abram's name to "Abraham."

Isaac grew in strength and beauty, and Abraham loved him very much. God wanted to test Abraham. The pagan cultures all around Abraham engaged in human sacrifice to their Gods. God wanted to see if Abraham loved him as much as the pagans loved their Gods, so he told Abram to sacrifice Isaac on an altar. Abraham took Isaac to Mount Moriah and prepared to offer him as sacrifice. Isaac himself carried the wood up the mountain for the sacrificial fire. Isaac was a "type" of Jesus, who carried his own wooden cross up Mount Calvary. Abraham bound Isaac, and prepared to offer sacrifice. But God sent an angel to stop Abraham's hand. God said to him: "Do not lay your hand on the lad or do anything to him; for now I know that you fear God, seeing that you have not withheld your son, your only son, from me." God provided Abraham with a lamb for sacrifice instead.

God renewed his covenant with Abraham, and promised to make him the "Father of many nations." This was the Third Covenant.

Isaac married Rebekah, and she gave birth to twin sons, Jacob and Essau. Essau came out of the womb first, but Jacob tricked Essau into renouncing his birthright. Jacob had twelve sons, and they became the Fathers of the Twelve Tribes of Israel.

But sin crept in to human history again and again. Jacob's favorite son was his youngest, Joseph. Joseph's brothers, out of jealousy, tried to kill him. He was saved by some passing nomads, and taken to Egypt. There he gained favor with the King of Egypt, and eventually rose to become Prime Minister. Years later, a famine came upon the land of Canaan, and Joseph's brothers were starving. They went to Egypt looking for food. Joseph was the Prime Minister of Egypt. He could have punished them for what they did to him, but he forgave them, reconciled with them and gave them the best land in Egypt, and they prospered.

Jacob's descendants multiplied and became very numerous in Egypt, but after a while there came a Pharaoh who did not know or remember the story of Joseph, and the descendants of Jacob were enslaved and treated very cruelly.

Eventually, there came a time when the Hebrews were so numerous that the Egyptians were afraid of them, even though they were slaves. So the Pharaoh ordered that the first-born son of every Hebrew be killed. But one Hebrew boy was saved when his mother put him in a basket made of reeds and sent it down the Nile River. It was found by Pharaoh's daughter, who named him "Moses," which means "I drew him out of the water," and she raised him as her own.

One day after he was an adult Moses saw an Egyptian beating a Hebrew, and he killed the Egyptian. But he was threatened by a fellow Israelite and was forced to flee for his life, and he went into the desert, where he took the daughter of Jethro, priest of Midian, as a wife and settled down. One day, while he was grazing his father-in-laws sheep, God appeared to him in a burning bush, and told him to go and lead his people out if slavery in Egypt. Initially, Moses did not want to go because he was afraid. But God promised to be with him, and to give him the words to speak. God said to Moses:

Say therefore to the people of Israel, 'I am the LORD, and I will bring you out from under the burdens of the Egyptians, and I will deliver you from their bondage, and I will redeem you with an outstretched arm and with great acts of judgment, and I will take you for my people, and I will be your God; and you shall know that I am the LORD your God, who has brought you out from under the burdens of the Egyptians. And I will bring you into the land which I swore to give to Abraham, to Isaac and to Jacob; I will give it to you for a possession. I am the LORD.[41]

In faith, Moses obeyed.

Initially, the Pharaoh refused to let the Hebrew People go, but God performed ten signs and wonders, and eventual Pharaoh agreed out of fear of the God of Moses. Then, when the Hebrews were on their way, Pharaoh repudiated his agreement and sent his army to kill them. God parted the Red Sea for the Israelites, and then made the waters return and drown the Egyptian army.

The Israelites wandered in the desert for forty years. It did not take them forty years to reach the promised land—they probably reached it in a few

---

[41] *Exodus 6:6-8.*

months. But they were afraid of the Canaanites who lived there, and did not trust in the Lord. So the Lord caused them to wander in the desert for forty years, until the unfaithful generation had died off, and a new generation, which was faithful and trusted in him, was raised up. The Hebrews were purified and chastised by God, and formed into a people. God fed them with manna and quail, and gave them water from a rock. He took Moses up to the top of Mount Sinai, and gave him the Ten Commandments. He inspired Moses to teach the people the *Shema*, that prayer of prayers that every devout Jew says at the beginning of every day:

Hear, O Israel: the LORD our God is one LORD, and you shall love the LORD your God with all your heart, and with all your soul, and with all your might. And these words which I command you this day shall be on your heart; and you shall teach them diligently to your children, and you shall talk of them when you sit in your house, and when you walk by the way, and when you lie down, and when you rise. And you shall bind them as a sign upon your hand, and they shall be as frontlets between your eyes. And you shall write them on the doorposts of your house and on your gates.[42]

God told Moses to choose seventy-two men and make them judges to rule over the people. He made Moses' brother Aaron and his sons and descendants priests, to offer sacrifice on behalf of the people. He made another covenant with Moses and the people — the Fourth Covenant. Eventually they were led across the Jordan River into the Promised Land by Joshua, where they conquered the Canaanites and settled down.

God gave them judges to rule and guide them, men and women of holiness and wisdom, like Deborah, Gideon, Samson and Samuel, who listened to the Word of God and sought to do his will. But

---

[42] *Deuteronomy 6:4-9.*

eventually they started to demand a king as other nations had. God told them that was a bad idea, but He gave them their wish and anointed Saul as their first king. Saul was not a good king. He abused the people, and they were not happy.

But when Saul was old, God selected David, a man after his own heart, to replace Saul. David was the youngest son of Jesse, the head of one of the smallest of the Hebrew Tribes. God told the judge and prophet Samuel, to anoint the son of Jesse whom God would choose. Samuel brought each of Jesse's sons to God in turn, but he rejected them, even though they were older and stronger than David. Finally, God told Samuel to anoint David, the youngest son. Repeatedly through Salvation History, as in the case of Jacob, of Joseph, of David, God rejected the older and wiser sons whom human wisdom would have selected, and chose the youngest and least likely. David loved God and ruled wisely, but even David succumbed to sin. He committed adultery with a woman named Bathsheba, and then tried to cover it up by sending her husband to the front lines in battle, where he was killed. But David repented and did penance, and he was forgiven. In repentance, he composed one of the greatest of the penitential Psalms, one that is sung and prayed in the Liturgy of the Hours:

Have mercy on me, O God, in your kindness,
In your compassion blot out my offense.
O wash me more and more from my guilt
And cleanse me from my sin.

My offenses truly I know them;
My sin is always before me.
Against you, you alone have I sinned;
What is evil in your sight I have done.

That you may be justified when you give sentence
And be without reproach when you judge,
O see, in guilt I was born,
A sinner was I conceived.

Indeed you love truth in the heart;

Then in the secret of my heart teach me wisdom.

O purify me, then I shall be clean;

O wash me, I shall be whiter than snow.[43]

God forgave David, and made another covenant with him, the Fifth Covenant, and God promised David that he would be the Father of a dynasty that would last forever.

The Hebrew people eventually broke faith with God again and apostasied, and God allowed them to be defeated in battle and carried off in slavery to Babylon. They were captive in Babylon for seventy years, during which time they reflected on their unfaithfulness, and came to realize that it was the cause of their tribulations. Then God sent Babylon a new king, Cyrus, who freed them and allowed them to return to Jerusalem. They rebuilt the temple, but they continued to lose faith, and were conquered in turn by the Greeks and the Romans.

---

[43] *Psalm 51.*

Finally, in the fullness of time, God carried out what was his plan from the beginning. He became man, took on human flesh, and atoned for the sin of Adam and Eve by suffering, dying and rising from the dead, thereby conquering sin and death. God sent an angel to a young virgin named Mary, to reveal to her that she had been chosen to be the Mother of God's Son—that she was to carry the eternal Word of God, the second person of the Blessed Trinity in her womb. In this way, God, in the person of Jesus Christ, took on human flesh. We call this "the incarnation." Incarnation comes from the Latin words "in + carne." "Carne" means flesh, so literally incarnation means "infleshment." Mary could have said "no," as did Eve, but she freely chose to do God's will, and said "Be it done unto me according to thy will." Through this "fiat," Mary gave Jesus his human nature, and became the Mother of God.

Mary is the New Eve. In contrast to Eve, who refused to do God's will, Mary completely submitted herself to God's will. Even though she didn't understand it and was likely afraid, she said "Let it be done unto me according to your will."[44] Mary is the only creature in human history created without original sin. God did this great favor for her, not due to her merit, but in anticipation of the merit of Jesus' sacrifice on the Cross, and in order that Jesus Christ, God become man, could enter human history through a pure, undefiled vessel.

Mary, although a virgin, gave birth to Jesus, the Son of God. He was born into the poorest of surroundings in a stable in Bethlehem, the City of David, to fulfill God's promise to David in the Covenant.

This is the crucial mystery of our faith, the fact that God took on human flesh, and became man, born of a virgin and conceived by the power of the Holy Spirit, and became one of us.

Jesus grew in wisdom and strength, and when He was about 30, He began his public ministry by submitting to baptism in the Jordan River by his cousin, John the Baptist. Then He selected twelve

---

[44] *Luke 1:38.*

men to be his apostles. All of this was done to fulfill what the prophets in the Old Testament had predicted about the Messiah.

In Jesus' public ministry, which lasted about three years, He performed many signs and wonders. He healed the sick, restored sight to the blind, hearing to the deaf, made the crippled walk. He raised the dead. He taught love and forgiveness and mercy. He instituted the sacraments.

He converted many, but the hearts of the leaders of the people were closed to Him, because He was a challenge to their power and status. Eventually, they denounced Him, and handed Him over to the Romans to be crucified, after subjecting Him to a sham trial, and torturing Him with whips and thorns.

He died a horrible, painful, ignominious death on the cross, and His body was laid in a tomb. But on the third day, He rose from the dead. During the next forty days, He was seen by many, appeared to the apostles often, and instructed them in the meaning of all they had seen and heard, and all that he had said and done during His public ministry. He explained to them the meaning of the mysteries of faith, and gave them the sacred *Deposit of Faith* that they were to hand on to their successors through oral teaching. He gave them a *Mystagogia,* a deeper understanding of what they had already experienced.

He gave them the authority to forgive sins, to heal the sick, to teach, to govern and to sanctify, and most important, to make his Body and Blood present to the assembly through the celebration of the sacred mysteries, the Sacrament of the Eucharist.

After forty days, he rose into heaven in their sight, after first instructing them to preach to all nations, baptizing them in the name of the Father and of the Son and of the Holy Spirit, and to preach the good news of salvation, first in Jerusalem, then in Judea and Samaria, and then to the ends of the earth.

He promised them that they would not be alone. He promised to send his Holy Spirit to watch over and guide them, to preserve them from error, and to be with them until the end of time. Eight days later, the Holy Spirit came upon them while they were praying in the Upper Room with Mary and the other disciples. The apostles immediately went out into the street, spoke in tongues, prophesied, healed the sick and preached; 3,000 were converted and baptized on that day. The Church was born, and will last forever.

CHAPTER EIGHT

THE CANON OF SCRIPTURE

—⁓—

The catechist must be prepared to deal with the question: "Where did we get the bible?" It comes up in a number of contexts. For one thing, the catechist should be aware of and know how to explain the fact that Protestants use a somewhat different bible than Catholics do. The Catholic bible contains 46 books in the Old Testament. The bible used by most Protestants contains only 39 books. The seven books which the Catholic Church recognizes as canonical and many Protestants do not are: Tobit, Judith, Wisdom, Sirach, Baruch, 1 Macabees, 2 Macabees, and small parts of Daniel and Esther.

The list of books contained in the bible is called the "Canon of Scripture." As we saw earlier, the word "canon" comes from a Greek word which means "rule" or "ruler" or "norm." In the early Christian Church it came to mean what is normative for the Church. In the Fourth Century, it came to mean the list of books officially recognized as comprising the bible, the Holy Scriptures. The same word is used in "Canon Law," which is the official list of the church's statutes, and "Canonization," which is the process of the Church adding a person to the list of officially recognized saints.[45]

The question also comes up in the context of the source of revealed truth. There are many who hold the theory of "*sola scriptura*," that is that scripture is the only source of revelation. The Catholic Church rejects sola scripture, and teaches that both Scripture and Tradition,— that is that body of teaching handed on by the apostles through the Pope as successor to St.

---

[45] *The Bible, the Church and Authority*, p. 60.

Peter and the bishops in communion with him (The Magisterium)—are both sources of revealed truth.

One of the ways we can demonstrate that Tradition is a source of revealed truth is to examine the questions of how and from whence we got the bible, because the answer is that we got the bible from the Church in the exercise of her teaching office, the Magisterium. The catechist should be familiar with at least the general outline of this story.

The Jews divided the Hebrew Scriptures (the Old Testament) into the three groupings: The Law, the Prophets and "The Writings." The Law, or the Torah, consisted of the first five books of the Old Testament: Genesis, Exodus, Leviticus, Numbers and Deuteronomy. By the term "Prophets" the Jews included the major and minor prophets as well as the historical books. "The Writings" referred to Psalms, Proverbs, Job, Canticle of Canticles, Ruth, Lamentations, Ecclesiastes, Esther, Daniel, Ezra and Nehemiah, Wisdom, Sirach and the Song of Solomon.

These "books" actually consisted at that time of individual scrolls which were circulated for reading at the prayer services in the synagogues. They were not collected into one body of literature until about the Second Century B.C. At that time 70 scholars— Greek-speaking Diaspora Jews working in the library in Alexandria, Egypt— translated all of the Hebrew Scriptures into Greek. This giant translation project produced a body of scriptures known as the "Septuagint" from a Greek word meaning "seventy." This translation and codification is often referred to in biblical literature as the "LXX," which are the Roman numerals for seventy.

It is important to note that the Septuagint was the collection of scripture which was in use at the time of Jesus and the apostles, and from which they quoted when they alluded to scripture. It was also the version used by St. Paul, St. Mark, St. Luke and other authors of the New Testament when they quoted from the Hebrew Scriptures. More than eighty percent of the Old Testament quotes in the New Testament are from the Septuagint.

In the year 70 A.D. the Jews rebelled against Roman rule, and the Roman Army put the rebellion down in a bloodbath. The Romans destroyed the City of Jerusalem and leveled the Temple. In an attempt to rebound from this traumatic experience and to develop a post-Temple worship, the Jews called a council at the City of Jamnia. The Pharisee party gained the upper hand at this council, and they expelled the Jewish Christians from the Temple. They repudiated the Septuagint, mainly because it was being used extensively by the Christians in their worship. They settled instead on a Palestinian canon which was actually of later origin, and which did not contain the seven books listed above.[46]

Meanwhile, the Gospels and epistles, or letters, written by Paul, Peter and other apostles, were circulating among the Christian Churches and were being

---

[46] *The Consuming Fire: A Christian Introduction to the Old Testament*, by Rev. Michael Duggan, (San Francisco, 1991) p. 28-30.

used in the Liturgy of the Word which was the first part of the Mass. Also circulating among some communities at that time were some pseudo-Gospels, such as the Gnostic Gospel of Thomas, as well as some other epistles, such as the First and Second Epistles of St. Clement of Rome, the Third Pope, to the Corinthians, the Epistle of Barnabas, and others.

By the Fourth Century, the Pope and the bishops saw the need to establish a "canon," or list, of books which are considered the inspired Word of God and therefore suitable for reading at the Mass. A series of Councils of the church took up this question, beginning with the Council of Rome. In 382 B.C. Pope St. Damasus I formally approved the declaration of this Council that there are 46 books in the Old Testament and 27 in the New Testament. The 73 books are in use in all Catholic bibles today. Confirming decrees were passed by the Council of Hippo in 393 B.C., (which was presided over by St. Augustine as Bishop of Hippo,) and the Council of Carthage in 419 B.C., which was confirmed by Pope Innocent I. It was again confirmed by the Seventh Ecumenical Council, Nicea II, in 787.[47]

The same canon was reaffirmed again by the Ecumenical Council of Florence in 1442, and was raised to the level of dogma by the Council of Trent in 1562. Dogma is the highest form of Church teaching. It is doctrine which the Church has formally declared to be contained in Revelation, and necessary for salvation. As the Catechism teaches, dogmas "obligate the Christian people to an irrevocable adherence of faith."[48]

This teaching was reaffirmed again by the Second Vatican Council, when it taught:

For the holy mother Church, relying on the belief of the Apostles (see John 20:31; 2 Tim 3:16; 2 Peter 1:19-20; 3:15-16), hold that the books of both the Old and New Testaments in

---

[47] *Answer Me This! By Patrick Madrid, (Huntington, IN, 2003),* p. 175.

[48] *CCC, #88.*

their entirety, with all their parts, are sacred and canonical because written under the inspiration of the Holy Spirit, they have God as their author and have been handed on as such to the Church herself.[49]

For over a thousand years, no one questioned the Catholic Canon of Scripture. It was accepted by all Christians. But at the time of the Protestant Reformation, when Martin Luther translated the Bible into German, he removed the seven Old Testament Books referred to above. He did this for two reasons. For one thing, these books contained biblical support for doctrines which he rejected. For example, the doctrine of Purgatory is contained in 2 Macabees, and the doctrine of grace through alms-giving, prayer and fasting is contained in the Book of Tobit. Luther rejected these doctrines. Secondly, he mistakenly thought that the Palestinian Canon

---

[49] *Dei Verbum #11.*

was older, and therefore purer, than the Septuagint. Actually the opposite is true.

The issue of the Canon of Scripture has great catechetical significance. The bible is the living Word of God. It should always be at the heart of any effort at catechesis, which is the handing on of faith through instruction, especially oral instruction. But the bible must be used in conjunction with and in the context of the living tradition of the Church. Pope John Paul II said in *Catechesi Tradendae*:

Catechesis will always draw its content from the living source of the Word of God transmitted in Tradition and the Scriptures, for "sacred Tradition and Sacred Scripture make up a single sacred deposit of the Word of God, which is entrusted to the Church," as was recalled by the Second Vatican Council, which desired that "the ministry of the Word—pastoral preaching, catechesis and all forms of Christian instruction...—(should be) healthily nourished and (should) thrive in holiness through the word of Scripture.[50]

But in order to use the bible in catechesis, we have to know and agree upon the writings which comprise the bible. It makes a difference whether there are 39 books in the Old Testament or whether there are 46. It is not a matter of indifference, and it is not a matter of opinion. It is a matter of doctrine. We must know how the doctrine developed, and be able to cite the authority for it.

The second reason that the issue is of catechetical significance is that there are important doctrines which have their biblical foundation in one or more of the seven disputed books. For example, the biblical foundation for the doctrine of Purgatory is in II Macabees 12:41-45; the doctrine of almsgiving as a salutary source of grace and penance is found in Tobit 4:7-11; the doctrine of God's universal love

---

[50] *Catechesi Tradendae (On Catechesis in Our Tme)*, by Pope John Paul II, para 27, p. 26-27.

and his will that all men be saved is found in the Book of Wisdom; and in the Book of Judith, we have a foreshadowing of the role of Mary. Old Testament scholar Michael Duggan points out:

> As a model of faith, Judith foreshadows Mary insofar as she does the will of God on behalf of the people. Uzziah's blessing on Judith fore-shadows Elizabeth's pronouncement that Mary is "Of all women...the most blessed (Luke 1:42; cf. Judith 13:18)...Judith's prayerful disposition and declaration of God's vindication of the lowly over the mighty foreshadow Mary's acclamation of praise for God's work of deliverance on behalf of the humble. (Luke 1:46-55; cf. Judith 9:11-12; 16:2-17).[51]

It is very important that catechists understand this issue and be able to explain it in very clear, concise, coherent terms.

---

[51] *The Consuming Fire*, p. 544.

CHAPTER NINE

THE MAGISTERIUM

—〰—

The word *Magisterium* means "teaching office." The *Magisterium* is the teaching office of the Church, not "office" in the sense of a place with desks and computers, but "office" in the sense of an authority. The word "office" is used here in the same sense as when we say "he holds the office of Governor" (or Mayor, or Judge). The Church has the authority to teach doctrine; that is to teach the revealed truths which we need to know for the sake of our salvation. The Church received that authority from Jesus himself, and she exercises it in His name. Jesus gave that authority to the Church before His ascension, and it is recorded in a number of places in the Scriptures:

He who hears you hears me, and he who rejects you rejects me, and who rejects me rejects him who sent me.

Luke 10:16

Truly I say to you, whatever you bind on earth shall be bound in heaven, and whatever you loose on earth shall be loosed in heaven.

Matthew 18:18

And Jesus answered him, blessed are you, Simon bar Jonah! For flesh and blood has not revealed this to you, but my father who is in heaven. And I tell you, you are Peter, and upon this rock I will build my Church, and the gates of Hell will not prevail against it. I will give you the keys of the kingdom of heaven, and whatever you bind on earth will be bound in heaven, and whatever you loose on earth shall be loosed in heaven.

Matthew 16:17-20.

These things I have spoken to you, while I am still with you. But the Holy Spirit, the Counselor, whom the Father will send in my name, he will teach you all things, and bring to your remembrance all that I have said to you. *John 14:26.*

Go therefore and make disciples of all nations, baptizing them in the name of the Father and of the Son and of the Holy Spirit, teaching them to observe all that I have commanded you; and lo, I am with you always, to the end of the age.
Matthew 28:20.

The purpose of the Magisterium or teaching office of the Church is to hand on the *Deposit of Faith*, as it was received from Jesus himself, the Divine Teacher, and handed down to us from the apostles and their successors. The *Deposit of Faith* never changes, but it is the case that it must be interpreted anew for each age, using terms that can be understood in the context of the present reality. This task of interpretation is the function of the Magisterium, guided by the Rule of Faith and the Standard of Faith.

The Magisterium enjoys the charism of infallibility. This means that it is protected from all error by the Holy Spirit, when it is teaching definitively a doctrine pertaining to faith or morals. The Catechism teaches:

> The task of giving an authentic interpretation of the Word of God, whether in its written form or in the form of tradition, has been entrusted to the living, teaching office of the Church alone. It's authority in this matter is exercised in the name of Jesus Christ. This means that the task of interpretation has been entrusted to the bishops in communion with the successor of Peter, the Bishop of Rome.[52]

---

[52] *CCC, #85.*

There are three ways in which the Church can exercise the charism of infallibility. They are:

1. When the Pope speaks *ex cathedra* (literally, "From the Chair") on a matter of faith or morals.

2. By a teaching of a Council of the Church, in a formal pronouncement, which by its terms is intended to be definitive, and **when confirmed or ratified by the Pope**.

3. When the Pope, and the bishops in communion with him dispersed throughout the world, agree that a doctrine is to be held definitively. This method is commonly used when the Pope, through an encyclical, apostolic letter or some other official pronouncement, confirms a doctrine previously taught by the Magisterium.

The last of these three ways of exercising infallibility is called the "Ordinary Magisterium," while the first two are referred to as the "Extraordinary

Magisterium." However, all are of equal stature and validity, and all are equally binding on the faithful.

There are some who erroneously argue that they only have to believe doctrines taught by the extraordinary Magisterium, but not those defined by the ordinary Magisterium. This is manifestly false. The term "ordinary" in "Ordinary Magisterium" refers to the fact that it is exercised in an ordinary way, i.e. the way normally used. The term "extraordinary" refers to the fact that *ex cathedra* pronouncements by the Pope and the councils of the Church are relatively rare. For example, there have only been 21 Ecumenical Councils in the entire two thousand year history of the Church, and there have only been two *ex cathedra* pronouncements in the last 150 years,[53] whereas statements from the Pope confirming the infallibility of previously taught doctrines are more common.

However, the important element to understand is that the response required from the faithful by all

---

[53] The Dogma of the Immaculate Conception in 1854, and the Dogma of the Assumption in 1950.

three methods of exercising the charism of infallibility, is the wholehearted *assent of faith*. The Second Vatican Council, in the Dogmatic Constitution on the Church, teaches:

> This infallibility, however, with which the divine redeemer wished to endow his Church in defining doctrine pertaining to faith and morals, is co-extensive with the deposit of revelation, which must be religiously guarded and loyally and courageously expounded. The Roman Pontiff, head of the college of bishops, enjoys this infallibility in virtue of his office, when as supreme pastor and teacher of all the faithful—who confirms his brethren in the faith (cf. Luke 22:32)—he proclaims in an absolute decision a doctrine pertaining to faith or morals. For that reason his definitions are rightly said to be irreformable by their very nature and not be reason of the assent of the Church, inasmuch as they were made

with the assistance of the Holy Spirit promised to him in the person of blessed Peter himself, and as a consequence they are in no way in need of the approval of others, and do not admit of appeal to any other tribunal. For in such a case the Roman Pontiff does not utter a pronouncement as a private person, but rather does he expound and defend the teaching of the Catholic faith as the supreme teacher of the universal Church, in whom the Church's charism of infallibility is present in a singular way.

...Furthermore, when the Roman Pontiff, or the body of bishops together with him, define a doctrine, they make the definition in conformity with revelation itself, to which all are bound to adhere and to which they are obliged to submit...

...Religious submission of will and of mind must be shown in a special way to the authentic teaching authority of the Roman Pontiff, even when he is not speaking *ex cathedra*. That is, it must be shown in such a way that his supreme Magisterium is acknowledged with reverence, the judgments made by him are sincerely adhered to, according to his manifest mind and will. His mind and will in the matter may be known chiefly either from the character of the documents, from his frequent repetition of the same doctrine, or from his manner of speaking.[54]

An example of the Pope speaking infallibly when exercising the Ordinary Magisterium by reaffirming a doctrine previously taught is the question of the ordination of women to the priesthood. In 1976, Pope Paul VI approved and published the Declaration *Inter*

---

[54] *Lumen Gentium, para. 25.*

Insigniores, declaring that the Church cannot ordain women to the ministerial priesthood.[55]

Despite this definitive statement, there were those within the Church who continued to treat this subject as if it were open for legitimate debate. Some were heard to characterize this definitive teaching as the "opinion of the Pope," subject to revision or change by a future Pope.

To put an end to all such speculation, on May 26, 1994, Pope John Paul II published the Apostolic Letter *Ordinatio Sacerdotalis,* in which he taught:

> Wherefore, in order that all doubt may be removed regarding a matter of great importance, a matter which pertains to the Church's divine constitution itself, in virtue of my ministry of confirming the brethren (cf. Luke 22:32) I declare that the Church has no authority whatsoever to confer priestly

---

[55] Congregation for the Doctrine of the Faith, Declaration Inter Insignores, (October 15, 1976), AAS 69, (1977), 98-116.

ordination on women and that this judgment is to be definitively held by all the Church's faithful.

This statement is direct, straightforward and devoid of any ambivalence whatsoever. It seems impossible that anyone could fail to understand its import, intent and gravity. However, some American theologians managed to do so. As a result, the U. S. Conference of Bishops sent a *Dubium*, or question, to the Congregation for the Doctrine of Faith, asking whether this teaching is to be understood as belonging to the Deposit of Faith. On October 28, 1995, Cardinal Joseph Ratzinger, Prefect of the Congregation for the Doctrine of the Faith, issued a response which had been approved and ordered published by the Pope himself. It said:

This teaching requires definitive assent, since, founded on the written Word of God, and from the beginning constantly preserved and applied in the Tradition of the Church, it has been set forth infallibly by the ordinary and universal Magisterium (cf. Second Vatican Council, Dogmatic Constitution on the Church, *Lumen Gentium* 25, 2). Thus, in the present circumstances, the Roman Pontiff, exercising his proper office of confirming the brethren (cf. Luke 22:32), has handed on this same teaching by a formal declaration, explicitly stating what is to be held always, everywhere, and by all, as belonging to the deposit of the faith.[56]

The above teaching, therefore, is infallible because it is a teaching handed on from earliest times, and confirmed by the Pope exercising the Ordinary Magisterium through the explicit exercise of a formal declaration, and explicitly stating that he

---

[56] *Responsum ad Dubium,* Sacred Congregation for the Doctrine of the Faith, Rome, October 28, 1995.

is exercising his ministry of confirming the brethren. The Code of Canon Law, §750.2 provides:

> Each and every thing which is proposed definitively by the Magisterium of the Church concerning the doctrine of faith and morals, that is, each and every thing which is required to safeguard reverently and to expound faithfully the same deposit of faith, is also to be firmly embraced and retained; therefore, one who rejects those propositions which are to be held definitively is opposed to the doctrine of the Catholic Church.

Canon 751 provides:

> Heresy is the obstinate denial or obstinate doubt after the reception of baptism of some truth which is to be believed by divine and Catholic faith;

And so, when the Magisterium, whether though the ministry of the Pope alone, or the Pope with the Bishops in communion with him, teaches on a matter of faith and morals in a manner which signifies that it is intended to be a definitive declaration, that act possesses the charism of infallibility, whether it is an act of the Ordinary Magisterium or of the Extraordinary Magisterium. Furthermore, all of the faithful are required to give the assent of faith to such teaching, and failure to do so constitutes an act of heresy,[57] and separates such a person from communion with the Church.

---

[57] *Code of Canon Law, §750(2).*

APPENDIX A

—〜〜—

On June 29, 1968, at the close of the Year of Faith, Pope Paul VI proclaimed the *Credo of the People of God*. In the Apostolic Letter transmitting the Credo, he stated that his purpose was to offer to the Christian world after the Second Vatican Council a profession of the principal articles of the Catholic faith, in order "to give witness to our steadfast will to guard the Deposit of Faith from corruption."

He called the *Credo of the People of God* "a carefully assembled synthesis of those revealed truths which today are either most challenged or that especially need to be understood by the faithful." He noted that it incorporates all the familiar doctrines of the Nicene Creed, "but goes beyond them in occasionally updating their verbal expression and showing how these mysteries are to be lived by the Christian believer."

Sadly, the *Credo of the People of God* never received as much attention or wide a dissemination as it should have. It is seldom taught in most Religious education or Theology programs, with a few notable exceptions. Printed copies are difficult to obtain even in the best Catholic book stores, although it is readily available on the internet, at the official Vatican website and others.

Because of its importance in refuting the secularism, atheism and nihilism of post-modern society, it is reproduced in its entirety in this appendix, and its use is strongly recommended to all catechists.

THE CREDO OF THE PEOPLE OF GOD

By His Holiness Pope Paul VI

Proclaimed on 30 June 1968

We believe in one only God, Father, Son and Holy Spirit, Creator of things visible such as this world in which our transient life passes, of things invisible such as the pure spirits which are also called angels (3), and Creator in each man of his spiritual and immortal soul.

We believe that this only God is absolutely one in His infinitely holy essence as also in all His perfections, in His omnipotence, His infinite knowledge, His providence, His will and His love. He is He who is, as He revealed to Moses (4), and He is love, as the apostle John teaches us (5): so that these two names, being and love, express ineffably the same divine reality of Him who has wished to make Himself

known to us, and who, "dwelling in light inacces-
sible" (6) is in Himself above every name, above
every thing and above every created intellect. God
alone can give us right and full knowledge of this
reality by revealing Himself as Father, Son and Holy
Spirit, in whose eternal life we are by grace called to
share, here below in the obscurity of faith and after
death in eternal light. The mutual bonds which eternally constitute the Three Persons, who are each one
and the same divine being, are the blessed inmost
life of God thrice holy, infinitely beyond all that we
can conceive in human measure (7). We give thanks,
however, to the divine goodness that very many
believers can testify with us before men to the unity
of God, even though they know not the mystery of
the most holy Trinity.

We believe then in the Father who eternally begets
the Son, in the Son, the Word of God, who is eternally
begotten; in the Holy Spirit, the uncreated Person
who proceeds from the Father and the Son as their

eternal love. Thus in the Three Divine Persons, *coae-ternae sibi et coaequales*, (8) the life and beatitude of God perfectly one superabound and are consummated in the supreme excellence and glory proper to uncreated being, and always "there should be venerated unity in the Trinity and Trinity in the unity"(9).

We believe in our Lord Jesus Christ, who is the Son of God. He is the Eternal Word, born of the Father before time began, and one in substance with the Father, homoousios to Patri (10), and through Him all things were made. He was incarnate of the Virgin Mary by the power of the Holy Spirit, and was made man: equal therefore to the Father according to His divinity, and inferior to the Father according to His humanity (11); and Himself one, not by some impossible confusion of His natures, but by the unity of His person (12).

He dwelt among us, full of grace and truth. He proclaimed and established the Kingdom of God and made us know in Himself the Father. He gave us His new commandment to love one another as He loved us. He taught us the way of the beatitudes of the Gospel: poverty in spirit, meekness, suffering borne with patience, thirst after justice, mercy, purity of heart, will for peace, persecution suffered for justice sake. Under Pontius Pilate He suffered —the Lamb of God bearing on Himself the sins of the world, and He died for us on the cross, saving us by His redeeming blood. He was buried, and, of His own power, rose on the third day, raising us by His resurrection to that sharing in the divine life which is the life of grace. He ascended to heaven, and He will come again, this time in glory, to judge the living and the dead: each according to his merits—those who have responded to the love and piety of God going to eternal life, those who have refused them to the end going to the fire that is not extinguished.

And His Kingdom will have no end.

We believe in the Holy Spirit, who is Lord, and Giver of life, who is adored and glorified together with the Father and the Son. He spoke to us by the prophets; He was sent by Christ after His resurrection and His ascension to the Father; He illuminates, vivifies, protects and guides the Church; He purifies the Church's members if they do not shun His grace. His action, which penetrates to the inmost of the soul, enables man to respond to the call of Jesus: Be perfect as your Heavenly Father is perfect (Mt. 5:48).

We believe that Mary is the Mother, who remained ever a Virgin, of the Incarnate Word, our God and Savior Jesus Christ (13), and that by reason of this singular election, she was, in consideration of the merits of her Son, redeemed in a more eminent manner (14), preserved from all stain of original sin (15) and filled with the gift of grace more than all other creatures (16).

Joined by a close and indissoluble bond to the Mysteries of the Incarnation and Redemption (17), the Blessed Virgin, the Immaculate, was at the end of her earthly life raised body and soul to heavenly glory (18) and likened to her risen Son in anticipation of the future lot of all the just; and we believe that the Blessed Mother of God, the New Eve, Mother of the Church (19), continues in heaven her maternal role with regard to Christ's members, cooperating with the birth and growth of divine life in the souls of the redeemed (20).

We believe that in Adam all have sinned, which means that the original offense committed by him caused human nature, common to all men, to fall to a state in which it bears the consequences of that offense, and which is not the state in which it was at first in our first parents—established as they were in holiness and justice, and in which man knew neither evil nor death. It is human nature so fallen stripped of the grace that clothed it, injured in its own natural powers and subjected to the dominion of death, that is transmitted to all men, and it is in this sense that every man is born in sin. We therefore hold, with the Council of Trent, that original sin, is transmitted with human nature, "not by imitation, but by propagation" and that it is thus "proper to everyone" (21).

We believe that Our Lord Jesus Christ, by the sacrifice of the cross redeemed us from original sin and all the personal sins committed by each one of us, so that, in accordance with the word of the apostle, "where sin abounded grace did more abound" (22).

We believe in one Baptism instituted by our Lord Jesus Christ for the remission of sins. Baptism should be administered even to little children who have not yet been able to be guilty of any personal sin, in order that, though born deprived of supernatural grace, they may be reborn "of water and the Holy Spirit" to the divine life in Christ Jesus (23).

We believe in one, holy, Catholic, and Apostolic Church built by Jesus Christ on that rock which is Peter. She is the Mystical Body of Christ; at the same time a visible society instituted with hierarchical organs, and a spiritual community; the Church on earth, the pilgrim People of God here below, and the Church filled with heavenly blessings; the germ and the first fruits of the Kingdom of God, through which the work and the sufferings of Redemption are continued throughout human history, and which looks for its perfect accomplishment beyond time in glory (24).

In the course of time, the Lord Jesus forms His Church by means of the sacraments emanating from His plenitude (25). By these she makes her members participants in the Mystery of the Death and Resurrection of Christ, in the grace of the Holy Spirit who gives her life and movement (26). She is therefore holy, though she has sinners in her bosom, because she herself has no other life but that of grace:

it is by living by her life that her members are sanctified; it is by removing themselves from her life that they fall into sins and disorders that prevent the radiation of her sanctity. This is why she suffers and does penance for these offenses, of which she has the power to heal her children through the blood of Christ and the gift of the Holy Spirit.

Heiress of the divine promises and daughter of Abraham according to the Spirit, through that Israel whose scriptures she lovingly guards, and whose patriarchs and prophets she venerates; founded upon the apostles and handing on from century to century their ever-living word and their powers as pastors in the successor of Peter and the bishops in communion with him; perpetually assisted by the Holy Spirit, she has the charge of guarding, teaching, explaining and spreading the Truth which God revealed in a then veiled manner by the prophets, and fully by the Lord Jesus. We believe all that is contained in the word of God written or handed down, and that the Church proposes for belief as divinely revealed, whether by a solemn judgment or by the ordinary and universal magisterium (27). We believe in the infallibility enjoyed by the successor of Peter when he teaches ex cathedra as pastor and teacher of all the faithful (28), and which is assured also to the episcopal body when it exercises with him the supreme magisterium (29).

We believe that the Church founded by Jesus Christ and for which He prayed is indefectibly one in faith, worship and the bond of hierarchical communion. In the bosom of this Church, the rich variety of liturgical rites and the legitimate diversity of theological and spiritual heritages and special disciplines, far from injuring her unity, make it more manifest (30).

Recognizing also the existence, outside the organism of the Church of Christ of numerous elements of truth and sanctification which belong to her as her own and tend to Catholic unity (31), and believing in the action of the Holy Spirit who stirs up in the heart of the disciples of Christ love of this unity (32), we entertain the hope that the Christians who are not yet in the full communion of the one only Church will one day be reunited in one flock with one only shepherd.

We believe that the Church is necessary for salvation, because Christ, who is the sole mediator and way of salvation, renders Himself present for us in His body which is the Church (33). But the divine design of salvation embraces all men, and those who without fault on their part do not know the Gospel of Christ and His Church, but seek God sincerely, and under the influence of grace endeavor to do His will as recognized through the promptings of their conscience, they, in a number known only to God, can obtain salvation (34).

We believe that the Mass, celebrated by the priest representing the person of Christ by virtue of the power received through the Sacrament of Orders, and offered by him in the name of Christ and the members of His Mystical Body, is the sacrifice of Calvary rendered sacramentally present on our altars. We believe that as the bread and wine consecrated by the Lord at the Last Supper were changed into His body and His blood which were to be offered for us on the cross, likewise the bread and wine consecrated by the priest are changed into the body and blood of Christ enthroned gloriously in heaven, and we believe that the mysterious presence of the Lord, under what continues to appear to our senses as before, is a true, real and substantial presence (35).

Christ cannot be thus present in this sacrament except by the change into His body of the reality itself of the bread and the change into His blood of the reality itself of the wine, leaving unchanged only the properties of the bread and wine which our senses perceive. This mysterious change is very appropriately called by the Church transubstantiation. Every theological explanation which seeks some understanding of this mystery must, in order to be in accord with Catholic faith, maintain that in the reality itself, independently of our mind, the bread and wine have ceased to exist after the Consecration, so that it is the adorable body and blood of the Lord Jesus that from then on are really before us under the sacramental species of bread and wine (36), as the Lord willed it, in order to give Himself to us as food and to associate us with the unity of His Mystical Body (37).

The unique and indivisible existence of the Lord glorious in heaven is not multiplied, but is rendered present by the sacrament in the many places on earth where Mass is celebrated. And this existence remains present, after the sacrifice, in the Blessed Sacrament which is, in the tabernacle, the living heart of each of our churches. And it is our very sweet duty to honor and adore in the blessed Host which our eyes see, the Incarnate Word whom they cannot see, and who, without leaving heaven, is made present before us.

We confess that the Kingdom of God begun here below in the Church of Christ is not of this world whose form is passing, and that its proper growth cannot be confounded with the progress of civilization, of science or of human technology, but that it consists in an ever more profound knowledge of the unfathomable riches of Christ, an ever stronger hope in eternal blessings, an ever more ardent response to the love of God, and an ever more generous bestowal of grace and holiness among men. But it is this same love which induces the Church to concern herself constantly about the true temporal welfare of men.

Without ceasing to recall to her children that they have not here a lasting dwelling, she also urges them to contribute, each according to his vocation and his means, to the welfare of their earthly city, to promote justice, peace and brotherhood among men, to give their aid freely to their brothers, especially to the poorest and most unfortunate. The deep solicitude of the Church, the Spouse of Christ, for the needs of men, for their joys and hopes, their griefs and efforts, is therefore nothing other than her great desire to be present to them, in order to illuminate them with the light of Christ and to gather them all in Him, their only Savior. This solicitude can never mean that the Church conform herself to the things of this world, or that she lessen the ardor of her expectation of her Lord and of the eternal Kingdom.

We believe in the life eternal. We believe that the souls of all those who die in the grace of Christ— whether they must still be purified in purgatory, or whether from the moment they leave their bodies Jesus takes them to paradise as He did for the Good Thief—are the People of God in the eternity beyond death, which will be finally conquered on the day of the Resurrection when these souls will be reunited with their bodies.

We believe that the multitude of those gathered around Jesus and Mary in paradise forms the Church of Heaven, where in eternal beatitude they see God as He is (38), and where they also, in different degrees, are associated with the holy angels in the divine rule exercised by Christ in glory, interceding for us and helping our weakness by their brotherly care (39).

We believe in the communion of all the faithful of Christ, those who are pilgrims on earth, the dead who are attaining their purification, and the blessed in heaven, all together forming one Church; and we believe that in this communion the merciful love of God and His saints is ever listening to our prayers, as Jesus told us: Ask and you will receive (40). Thus it is with faith and in hope that we look forward to the resurrection of the dead, and the life of the world to come.

Blessed be God Thrice Holy. Amen.

Notes

1. 1 Tim 6:20.

2. Cf Luke 22:32.

3. Cf Dz.-Sch. 3002.

4. Cf E~.3:14.

5. I Jn. 4:8.

6. I Tim. 6:16.

7. Cf Dz.-Sch. 804.

8. Cf Dz.-Sch. 75.

9. ibid.

10. Cf Dz.-Sch. 150.

11. Cf Dz.-Sch.76.

12. Ibid.

13. Cf Dz.-Sch. 251-252.

14. Cf Lumen Gentium, 53.

15. Cf Dz.-Sch. 2803.

16. Cf Lumen Gentium, 53.

17. Cf Lumen Gentium, 53, 58, 61.

18. Cf Dz.-Sch. 3903.

19. Cf Lumen Gentium, 53, 58, 61, 63; Cf Paul VI, Alloc. for the Closing of the Third Session of the Second Vatican Council: AAS LVI [1964] 1016; Cf. Exhort. Apost. Signum Magnum, Introd.

20. Cf Lumen Gentium, 62; cf Paul VI, Exhort. Apost. Signum Magnum, p 1, n. 1.

21. Cf Dz.-Sch. 1513.

22. Rom. 5:20.

23. Cf Dz.-Sch. 1514.

24. Cf. Lumen Gentium, 8, 5.

25. Cf Lumen Gentium, 7, 11.

26. Cf Sacrosanctum Concilium, 5, 6; cf Lumen Gentium, 7, 12, 50.

27. Cf Dz.-Sch.3011.

28. Cf Dz.-Sch. 3074.

29. Cf Lumen Gentium, 25.

30. Cf. Lumen Gentium, 23; cf Orientalium Ecclesiarum 2, 3, 5, 6.

31. Cf Lumen Gentium, 8.

32. Cf Lumen Gentium, 15.

33. Cf Lumen Gentium, 14.

34. Cf Lumen Gentium, 16.

35. Cf Dz.-Sch. 1651.

36. Cf Dz.-Sch. 1642,1651-1654; Paul VI, Enc. Mysterium Fidei.

37. Cf S.Th.,111,73,3.

38. I Jn. 3:2; Dz.-Sch. 1000.

39. Cf Lumen Gentium, 49.

40. Lk. 10:9-10;Jn. 16:24

APPENDIX B

THE TEACHING PROGRAM OF THE APOSTLES AND FATHERS

—⟋⟍—

The Twelve Articles of the Creed

1. I believe in God, the Father Almighty, Creator of heaven and earth;

2. And in Jesus Christ, His only Son, Our Lord;

3. Who was conceived by the Holy Spirit; born of the Virgin Mary;

4. Suffered under Pontius Pilate, was crucified, died and was buried;

5. He descended into Hell; on the third day He rose again from the dead;

6. He ascended into Heaven: sitteth at the right hand of God, the Father Almighty;

7. From thence He shall come to judge the living and the dead.

8. I believe in the Holy Spirit;

9. The Holy Catholic Church,; the Communion of Saints;

10. The forgiveness of sins;

11. The resurrection of the body;

12. Life everlasting. Amen.

The Ten Commandments

1. I am the Lord your God. You shall have no other Gods before me.

2. You shall not take the name of the Lord your God in vain.

3. Remember to keep holy the Sabbath Day.

4. Honor your Father and your Mother.

5. You shall not kill.

6. You shall not commit adultery.

7. You shall not steal.

8. You shall not bear false witness against your neighbor.
9. You shall not covet your neighbor's wife.
10. You shall not covet your neighbor's goods.

The Seven Sacraments

1. Baptism.
2. Confirmation.
3. Eucharist.
4. Reconciliation.
5. Matrimony.
6. Holy Orders.
7. The Sacrament of the Sick.
8.

The Seven Petitions of the Lord's Prayer

Our Father:

1. Hallowed be Thy Name.
2. Thy Kingdom come.
3. Thy will be done.
4. Give us this day our daily bread.

5. Forgive us our trespasses.

6. Lead us not into temptation.

7. Deliver us from evil.

9 781602 664265